My Journey Through

FIBROMYALGIA

Rumors, Ravages & The Rescue

Nancy Alexander

with Laura Hodges Poole

My Journey through Fibromyalgia
Rumors, Ravages, and the Rescue

All physician names have been changed to respect the identity of those I sought treatment from during my illnesses.

Acknowledgements

Mother
Who found supernatural strength beyond her capabilities
to care for me and our boys when I became sick.

Ma-Ma
Who shared her love of beauty making me
feel special, gifted and talented.

Aunt Louise
She always listened to my thoughts
and ideas with love and encouragement.

Steve
My strength and encourager in the writing of this book.
The love of my life, my knight in shining armor
now, always and forevermore.

My Boys
Despite fears of how my illness would affect them. Our boys
are now loving husbands, fathers, and faithful men of God.

Laura, my co-writer
A friend to whom I could pour out the contents
of my heart, who knew all the right words to help
express my deepest thoughts & feelings.

"Dedicated to every person behind every name on the hundreds of emails I received, seeking my understanding and commiseration of their own debilitating illnesses.

The pile was too big (and growing way too fast) to answer each of you individually.

Here is what I would have told all and each of you."

And now these three remain: faith, hope and love.
But the greatest of these is love.

1 CORINTHIANS 13:13

Contents

Introduction

And after you have suffered a little while, the God of all grace, who has called you to His eternal glory in Christ, will Himself restore, confirm, strengthen and establish you.

1 PETER 5:10 ESV

For almost twenty-five years, I fought with every ounce of strength in my body before finally getting correctly diagnosed with and receiving proper medical care for fibromyalgia, which is defined as a "chronic disorder characterized by widespread pain, tenderness, and stiffness of muscles and associated connective tissue structures that is typically accompanied by fatigue, headache, and sleep disturbances."[1]

When I read through e-mails from other fibromyalgia sufferers, my heart breaks for the people living with extreme physical pain, emotional anguish, withdrawal, and even disbelief from doctors, friends, and family when they develop this mysterious ailment. The diagnosis of fibromyalgia is more common today than when I got sick decades ago, but many people suffer for years before receiving proper treatment. Some never do.

Worse yet is the stigma associated with this disease. Because the symptoms of chronic pain and weakness are not visible or definable, sufferers are often met with skepticism.

When I read these e-mails, I think: When are these ladies going to receive the understanding and belief that they really are sick? Where is the sympathy and help from their family along with the top notch medical care they need and deserve from doctors in our medically advanced country? After all, it's the twenty-first century!

Fibromyalgia is not in the sufferer's head. Nor is it something they can will themselves to get over. Fibromyalgia has finally been classified as a real medical disorder. However, a proper diagnosis can be elusive depending on the medical care received. Other illnesses can mimic or coexist with fibromyalgia, such as multiple sclerosis, lupus, rheumatoid arthritis, and celiac disease.

I get angry knowing the despair and hopelessness these people suffer as they fight a battle for their very lives. Someone needs to tell them they are *not crazy.* Someone needs to explain to their spouses, children, and friends that they need respect and comfort, and that medical care exists that can confirm their illness with a correct diagnosis. And then it hit me—*I am that someone!* God has chosen me to tell my story, no matter how painful, so I can make a difference in their lives.

If I had been diagnosed with a recognized disease, people would have believed I was sick. I would have been treated differently. But in 1980, people didn't believe me. They thought my illness was in my head. Worse yet, the doctors from whom I sought treatment didn't believe I had a real physical illness. Finding a doctor who's willing to listen and work diligently to eliminate or confirm the presence of other disorders is imperative.

Okay, Nancy ... calm down. Today is not 1980. Fibromyalgia has been proven, without a doubt, to be a disease—a horrible, debilitating disease that not only hurts the person who has it but everyone they interact with and particularly those they love. A chronic disease of any type affects the entire family.

The shame and embarrassment I felt for so many years was a needless tragedy. Yet the stigma involved with the diagnosis of fibromyalgia, coupled with the cocktail of medications well-intentioned doctors prescribe, often prevent a sufferer from finding their way back to wellness.

But now, I can actually thank God for the path my illness led me on. Battling fibromyalgia prepared me to be able to touch so many lives—the lives of people I have never met. It has led me to become an encouragement, a help, and a supporter of women who are suffering. I can reach out to them in love. I can tell them they are not alone because someone—this someone—understands and cares.

> But [the Lord] said to me, "My grace is sufficient for you, for my power is made perfect in weakness." Therefore I will boast all the more gladly about my weaknesses, so that Christ's power may rest on me. That is why, for Christ's sake, I delight in weaknesses, in insults, in hardships, in persecutions, in difficulties. For when I am weak, then I am strong.
>
> 2 CORINTHIANS 12:9-10

Although the majority of my mail is from women, this book is not just for women. Of the five million Americans suffering with fibromyalgia, 80 to 90 percent are women. Men and children comprise the other 10 to 20 percent.[2] In this book, I share useful information that can be applied to both genders.

Within the last ten years, I learned celiac disease can trigger fibromyalgia and that I have had celiac disease since birth. Celiac is defined as "a chronic hereditary intestinal disorder in which an inability to absorb the gliadin portion of gluten results in the gliadin triggering an immune response that damages the intestinal mucosa."[3] And since gluten is found in everything from oatmeal to medicine to makeup, those with celiac disease have a difficult time adjusting to the need for a gluten-free diet.

I had to do the research and find out what was wrong with me … while fighting a battle all alone. Did you hear that? *I* did the research. It's your body. Don't ever give up the battle to find answers to your medical problems and where to obtain treatment.

The double whammy of fibromyalgia and celiac disease almost destroyed me. It did destroy the quality of my life and impacted those around me for many years. While the journey through and then out of the clutches of fibromyalgia has been a difficult one—marked by physical and mental debilitation, and years of searching—excellent psychotherapy has allowed me to release some of the anger I carried for years about this issue.

During this time, I learned the true meaning of forgiveness and experienced God's healing touch on my body and soul. For whatever reasons, He allowed me to suffer this trial of brokenness, I may never fully understand this side of heaven. One thing I do finally now understand is that His grace is sufficient—even on the darkest days.

This is my story about the rumors I endured as people whispered around me, the ravages of the disease on my health and family, and the rescue that is possible with proper diet and medical care, and the love and support of a wonderfully caring family.

My God-inspired goal is to help those of you suffering from fibromyalgia get the proper care you need and deserve. I hope in sharing my story that you find commonality with your own struggles. My greatest desire is, after you've read this, you'll be able to gain a new perspective of fibromyalgia and its impact on your life, and then come away with new tools to lessen that impact as you move toward wellness.

God bless,

Nancy Alexander

So we fix our eyes not on what is seen, but on what is unseen,
since what is seen is temporary, but what is unseen is eternal.

2 CORINTHIANS 4:18

Prologue

– February, 1980

*M*y morning began like any other. The weather was cold and brisk, so I didn't look forward to going out in it. But at the top of my to-do list was buying groceries for my family. Though I had battled stomach problems and fatigue most of my life, my health had reached a point where even the most routine task I tried to do was a major undertaking.

I didn't want to ask my husband Steve to shop after he'd worked all day, although many times he did just that. I already felt guilty for choosing not to work outside the home after our sons were born. Steve hadn't said it in so many words, but I knew he didn't agree with my decision.

Determined to be a good wife and mother and contribute financially to the family, I began couponing. Couponing then was totally different than it is now. I had three drawers in a file cabinet filled with UPC codes torn from any product we purchased. By sending these to the manufacturer, I received coupons back in the mail. I often had so many coupons for items, I got money back or the item for free. The downside of my massive couponing was the inordinate amount of time it took to shop. I would be worn out by the time I checked out and headed home.

Overwhelmed by the thought of taking two toddlers into the grocery store with a long grocery list and stack of coupons, I called my mother. She had shopping of her own to do, so she agreed to go and help with the boys. For some reason unknown to me, this was a particularly hard day, physically as well as mentally. Later, I regretted pushing myself. Maybe if I'd stayed home, circumstances would have been different, I thought.

By the time we finished shopping, I was exhausted. Mother got in one checkout line with one of the boys and I in another. I waited patiently while the customer in front of me finished and the clerk began to check my items. The longer I stood there, the worse I felt. My heart pounded as a sense of dread and fatigue washed over me. Thoughts of panic raced through my mind. Should I leave my buggy, take one child and sit in the car? Why am I feeling this way? Why doesn't the check-out girl hurry? She is taking way too long. Why won't my heartbeat slow down? Am I going to pass out, or worse yet, have a heart attack?

I said to myself: "Think quickly, think quickly—something bad is going to happen."

I finally asked for a chair so I could sit. My stress eased enough that I could wait while my groceries were checked out and bagged. Mother got my groceries, the boys, and me into the car and drove us home.

I spent the next several weeks alternating between lying on the couch and the bed, with Mother, Steve, or Steve's mom there to help. What we initially thought was a virus turned out to be the tipping point for my undiagnosed celiac disease and onset of fibromyalgia. But none of us knew that then.

Meanwhile, I floundered, desperate to regain my health. Weeks dragged into months. Months dragged into years.

Everyone's patience wore thin. Steve had to work. Somehow I had to manage.

I pleaded with God to help me. Show me what I did wrong. Show me what I can do to be forgiven. Please God, I'll do whatever it takes.

As dark as those days were, I didn't realize at the time it was only the beginning of decades of debilitation. Darker days loomed ahead.

One day in particular.

A day that almost destroyed my marriage, undermined my emotional stability, and shook the very foundation of my faith.

Chapter One

Do not be anxious about anything, but in every situation, by prayer and petition, with thanksgiving, present your requests to God. And the peace of God, which transcends all understanding, will guard your hearts and your minds in Christ Jesus.

PHILIPPIANS 4:6-7

As far back as I can remember, I've felt broken. My earliest childhood memories are marked with bouts of sickness and loneliness. Mother stayed overwhelmed caring for my younger twin sisters, Sandra and Susan. Daddy worked long hours and then worked in the yard all day on Saturdays.

I grew up in Anderson, South Carolina, a little town in the upstate of South Carolina between Atlanta, Georgia, and Charlotte, North Carolina. On the surface, my family lived a typical Southern lifestyle in the 1950s. The traditional roles of homemaking and childrearing fell on my mother's shoulders. With three young children on her hands, Mother didn't have the time or energy to make sure I received equal attention from her as women today strive for with their children. This lack of interaction touched every facet of my life.

When I began elementary school, I had little success finding playmates. I felt like an outsider, much like I did at home. The fact that I failed to thrive in my environment and didn't have friends

wasn't nearly as important to my parents as my behavior. So I faded into my surroundings and caused those around me as little trouble as possible.

Many times during my childhood, I'd play by myself in a corner of our backyard. Daddy had built a storage building in front of a large fig tree. Behind the large fig tree was a dark, shady spot surrounded by many tall pine trees planted closely together where I could go and sit on the ground or sometimes on an old cement block. I could hear laughter from Sandra and Susan, and even neighbor children, as the back screen door slammed behind them when they ran in and out of the house.

As I grew older, I ventured out and discovered some boys to play with in my neighborhood. So I became somewhat of a tomboy. I learned not to be afraid of hard work, bugs, and worms.

My dad had a green thumb and always had the most beautiful thick grass in his yard along with gorgeous azaleas. He grew and multiplied Hosta plants, giving many away to friends.

Daddy's love of nature and creating things were the two things we had in common. Though I was an adult before I fashioned unique rustic wreaths adorned with birdhouses, birds, critters, and nests, creating with my hands was not only a God-given talent but something I learned from my father and from my dear grandmother. Being in the midst of nature comforted me.

As I grew older, I made three good friends—Beth, Emily, and Gail. Beth and Emily lived close enough for me to walk to their houses, but Gail didn't, so I didn't get to see her as much. Mother found it difficult to load her three children into the car to take me to a friend's house.

My feelings of alienation within my family and physical sickness persisted. At twelve years old, I was rushed to the emergency room on at least two occasions with severe stomachaches and body pain. The doctors thought it was appendicitis. When they discovered it wasn't, they sent me home. I had these severe stomachaches often. The pain was so intense, I couldn't even touch my stomach. I lay on the couch as still as possible while life went on around me in our little house.

Mother and Daddy grew accustomed to these attacks. After the first few emergency room visits, they believed my illness was nothing serious. Despite their reassurances that I wasn't dying, I dreaded the attacks. I couldn't move—I hurt so much.

I attended T. L. Hanna High School, now one of the largest and most academically prestigious schools in the Southeast. It was much smaller then, though cliquish as most schools tend to be. I didn't fit into the popular or wealthy kid cliques since I came from an average middle-class family.

Daddy worked for Duke Power. He had carefully saved and invested in their stock for our education. Since he'd dropped out of school after the third grade, it became his mission to see that his girls went to college. More specifically, we were to become teachers. I hated the idea. I had no interest in teaching others what I had a difficult time grasping myself. The one area I excelled in was art. That's all I was interested in doing with my life.

My high school art teacher, Mr. Merk, called my parents in for a parent-teacher meeting one day after school. He insisted my dad come too. Daddy actually got off early from work, which was unusual because he didn't get off early to attend school functions. Mr. Merk had one of my paintings showcased on an easel in his classroom for my parents to see. He talked with them about my talent and encouraged them to make sure I attended a college where I could major in art. Mr. Merk understood my love of art—and the dream that went along with it.

Mother and Daddy listened a short while. Then Daddy spoke. No, he couldn't afford to send me away to a school where I could major in art. I'm sure it hurt him to say these words, because he worked so hard to provide for a family of five. My parents were polite but firm. I was crushed. My art teacher recognized my talent, but I couldn't go to school to develop that talent.

On the way home, Daddy made it very clear I would be lucky to attend our small home-town college. His Duke Power stock had plummeted with the drop of the stock market. He didn't want to sell any of it for my college expenses because he'd be selling at almost half of what he had paid for it.

The subject was closed. Daddy's decision was final.

With my teen years came a freedom I didn't have before. I often went home after school with my friends. Sometimes I went to my grandmother's house after school. We sat on her front porch together in the afternoons watching the hummingbirds, which came by at four o'clock every day as we talked and enjoyed each other. Grandmother had always shown an interest in my thoughts and dreams for the future. She encouraged me and taught me how to sew, crochet, and paint my fingernails. Once I drew and painted a picture she considered exceptional, so she paid for art lessons. She also paid for me to take baton and dancing lessons: tap, ballet, and ballroom.

Mother's sister, Aunt Louise, and her husband, Uncle Harold, never had any children, so they doted on me. They took me on vacation every summer. These were happy times during my childhood and early teens. I felt loved and wanted when I was with them. Aunt Louise had pernicious anemia all of her life, and Uncle Harold had to give her B-12 shots every day. She carried something sweet along with saltine crackers in her pocketbook for when she had one of her "weak spells."

Looking back now, I believe Aunt Louise had celiac disease and possibly fibromyalgia. Mother also had all the symptoms of gluten sensitivity. I only wish someone had been able to diagnose them. Living with these illnesses myself, I understand better my mother's inability to show me the attention I craved. She had no energy left after two hard pregnancies and three children to care for.

Mother was high strung, got upset and cried easily, and didn't eat much. From a child's perspective, I didn't understand how much this colored her mood and the way she treated me. Her lack of affection and attention had a tremendous impact on my self-esteem and self-worth. I actually thought she hated me, but she was just sick. It's such a shame. I only wish I'd known.

After I graduated from high school, my parents chose Anderson College, a private Baptist college, for me to attend. Given the decreased value of Daddy's Duke Power stock, my parents turned to Aunt Louise and Uncle Harold to borrow the money to send me to Anderson College. Living on campus was out of the question because of the cost. The smaller school was more manageable than Clemson University or another large university. Although it was a nice school, I disliked being at Anderson College, mainly because it hadn't been my choice.

How could I become a teacher? The only subject I excelled in was art. I was horrible in math and history, though I managed in the other subjects.

At fourteen, I had started working at a nearby bakery after school and on weekends. I continued this job in college. The owners loved me and the work I did there showed them my love for art and design. They trained me to decorate birthday and wedding cakes. They knew I was unhappy at Anderson College and offered to pay for the college of my choice if I would agree to take over the bakery, managing it for them after graduation.

That was such a kind offer, but I knew I couldn't be happy working in a bakery as a career. I graduated from Anderson College two years later with an associate's degree and then transferred to Clemson University, about twenty miles from Anderson. I lost hours when I transferred. I attended Clemson for two years, including both summers but still needed more courses to graduate. Discouraged and unhappy, I quit. So after four years of college, I walked away with my associate of arts degree.

To say Daddy wasn't happy with me is an understatement. Being the oldest, I'm sure he had expectations I didn't fulfill. He didn't understand my artistic side, and I couldn't follow through on his academic desires for me. Skilled with his hands, he could take apart and put things back together, but amazingly he couldn't see that I shared this trait.

Part of this, I'm sure, was the fact that Daddy had nothing growing up. He was blessed to have gotten a job at Duke Power. He wanted to secure my sisters' and my future through education. Daddy dreamed big for his daughters, which was the crux of the problem. My college career had been his dream—not mine. There wasn't room in his dreams for my desires.

I didn't have a clue what I would do for a career, but I did know I wouldn't be teaching school. And my college years weren't a total loss. Skilled to work in a business office, I looked for a job. I'd also made a new friend, Janice Dickson, at Anderson College. Janice, Gail, and I hung out together, often at my house, talking about guys and our future as girls do.

Sometimes the three of us would go to McDonald's, a popular hot spot for teens. Those with cars cruised around the parking lot, while others stood outside talking. Janice, Gail, and I circled around twice before Janice spotted two boys she'd gone to high school with, one of which was a Clemson engineering student, Steve Alexander. Janice pulled in next to them and started talking across Gail through the open window. The guys got out of the car. Janice introduced us and asked if they wanted to ride around with us.

Steve got in the car quickly and slid over to the middle. Jerry slid in next to him. I was already in the backseat. Steve told me later that he was happy he got to the car door before Jerry so he could be the one to slide in beside me. When he first saw me, he thought I was cute and really liked me. We rode around for a while talking and then came back to McDonald's. I don't think we ever did eat.

Steve and I talked to each other more than the others. I thought Steve was really cute too. He had a charming smile and beautiful eyes that sparkled regardless of whether or not he was smiling. We chatted about Clemson, and he told me about attending Crescent High in Iva.

I have always thought "love at first sight" could not be real. It's infatuation in the moment, in a look or a smile. It definitely could not be the everlasting type of true love that takes time to grow and nurture from deep within your soul. But that night, I felt true love—there was no doubt in my heart we would grow old together. I saw it in his sweet smile, his laughing eyes, and the way he looked deeply into my own very existence. That was the day I personally experienced love at first sight, in the backseat of a car, sitting shoulder to shoulder with someone I had never met before—knowing we would be together always.

Janice later confided that Steve had been popular at Crescent. He'd been the quarterback on the football team, ran track, played baseball, and was captain of the basketball team. He went to Boy's State and had been one of the top two or three in his graduating class. He attended Clemson to take advantage of their nationally recognized engineering program. He was a Christian with several scholarships and very involved in his church. I didn't need to be impressed since I had just experienced "love at first sight," but I was.

My heart brimmed with happiness. When the boys finally got out of the car, Steve leaned in and looked at me with his smiling eyes and asked me for a date. Of course, I said yes. We made plans for the following Friday, after I gave him my phone number.

When the girls dropped me off a little later, Mother was waiting in my bedroom, as she always did anytime I went out. Sometimes I felt like I could open up and talk to her, other times not. This was one night I felt like sharing my happiness. I told her about meeting Steve.

Mother began fussing almost immediately, saying "good girls" don't do stuff like cruising and looking for boys. I told her how cute Steve was. He'd been so nice. He'd shared how involved he was in church, sang in choir, and had been a Boy Scout. I told her all of it. Then I looked her in the eye and said, "I have met the one that I will marry one day."

Well, this just about sent her over the edge. She kind of laughed and said, "You can't say that. You don't know that. You don't know anything about him."

"Yeah, I do," I said. "I just know he's the one for me."

Steve called several times during the week, and we talked for hours on the phone. The following Friday, he picked me up for our first date. He didn't tell me his plans ahead of time. He was taking me home to meet his parents. Overwhelmed, I didn't know what to say, so I just smiled and agreed. We drove out to his parents' house in Iva, a very small town that lies about fifteen miles south of Anderson, and had a nice conversation with his folks in their den. They did their best to put me at ease as we talked about family and got to know each other. Afterwards we went to his high school for a football game where I met his friends.

After that, we dated every weekend. Steve didn't have a car, so he used his parents' car to take me out. Phone calls from Clemson were long distance, so he hitched a ride or walked to Pendleton, a small town outside of Clemson, to use a pay phone to call me during the week.

This was also the start of many beautiful love letters we sent to each other, several times a week. We spent hours talking about the future—our hopes, dreams, and plans.

My home life was still tenuous. Mother never seemed to feel well. She weighed less than a hundred pounds. I often had back pain and didn't feel well either. But this was supposed to be the most carefree years of my life, and in a way, they were. I was young and in love. That eclipsed everything else.

During this time, I got a job at Clemson University in extension marketing where we produced peach reports for the farmers. Some days I'd walk to the canteen and eat lunch with Steve. I drove a 1966 Dodge Charger that Daddy had signed for me to make payments on. I joked with Steve that he was as interested in the car as he was me. Every day, Steve waited on me after work and we'd drive to the YMCA beach in Clemson and talk about life and our future. Steve made me feel special, giving me his undivided attention and smiling with a gleam in his eyes, like I was the center of his universe.

On the weekends, we went out to eat or to the movies. We would end up back at home, sitting on the couch in the den. Almost every time, Steve would fall asleep on the couch, and then Daddy would come in about midnight and say, "Son, you've gotta go home." And then we'd stand by the door and chat for a few minutes before Steve finally left.

Steve and I would join Gail and her boyfriend, Lewis, to play tennis. Sometimes we'd meet up with them and Janice at Lewis' parents' little one-room cabin on the lake. We water-skied, fished, and swam. We had so much fun!

Although I suffered with some back pains and stomachaches during this period, it wasn't enough to keep me down. I knew how far I could push myself and when to back off in order to maintain at least some balance in my health. I became very good at hiding my feelings. I didn't talk about my health, except maybe with Steve some, but even he didn't know how I really felt. I just didn't want anyone to know. That would mean I wasn't "okay" (whatever that is), and I wanted to be normal with no problems, enjoying the carefree existence all my friends seemed to enjoy. I'd go home from work and take a nap before our dates on Friday nights. I was careful about my diet and didn't eat much at all, though I had no idea how much of a role nutrition played in my health.

Steve and I kind of naturally started talking about spending our lives together, what we would do, where we would live, how many children we wanted, before he ever really asked me to marry him.

The first time I told him I loved him, he didn't respond. I thought, *Oh no*, I shouldn't have said that. I spoke too soon.

A couple of weeks later, we were sitting in a movie theater, watching *Tora, Tora, Tora*, and Steve told me he loved me. I'm not sure why he picked that particular moment, but he did. He told me later he loved me and wanted to spend the rest of his life with me, but marriage was a very big decision. He prayed about it and wanted to make sure before he told me he loved me.

After dating for nearly two years, while Steve was finishing Clemson and I worked for the Department of Social Services, Steve asked Daddy for my hand in marriage. Steve respected Daddy a great deal, and Daddy considered Steve the son he'd never had. Of course, Daddy said yes.

Steve and I rented a small house on East North Avenue, now Murray Avenue, in an older section of Anderson. I was so proud of that little house, but we had to fix it up before we could move into it after our wedding. Mother planned the wedding, but I painted and decorated the house. I wanted it to be perfect.

Mother and I picked out my wedding dress together at a shop in downtown Anderson. Beautifully trimmed with lace, it made me feel beautiful when I put it on. I remember Steve's face as I walked down the aisle toward him. His face beamed with pride and joy. I knew he loved me.

Steve's mother gave us a wedding present of a new bedroom set. We furnished the rest of the house with used or hand-made furniture, which I painted and decorated. We put very old green and white lounge chairs and an old TV in the den. Steve's mother also gave us an old drop-leaf table that she and Steve's dad used when they got married. I painted it yellow and antiqued it. My Aunt Marian still had some of grandmother's furniture in a storage building, so she let us have matching chairs.

Daddy got a large wooden power line reel left over from his work. We cut a circular piece of plywood bigger than the top and attached it to the top. I painted the whole thing bright yellow and glued fringe around the rim. Four ladder-back chairs, which completed our cute eating area, were the only things we bought for the house. The mix-and-match furniture sounds tacky now, but we didn't care. The little house was our own special place.

On July 15, 1972, we got married. Life couldn't have been better. I had married my best friend. Steve was attentive, loving, and nurturing. We returned from our honeymoon in Gatlinburg, Tennessee, a week later and moved into our new home. The future lay brightly ahead of us, and for the first time in my life, I felt happy, complete, and full of hope.

Chapter Two

In the same way, the Spirit helps us in our weakness.
We do not know what we ought to pray for, but the Spirit himself
intercedes for us with groans that words cannot express.

ROMANS 8:26

Steve graduated from Clemson University shortly after we married and took a job as a civil engineer with the South Carolina Highway Department. I worked as a social worker at the Department of Social Services. We both worked long hours. I often missed work due to epigastric and lower abdominal pain and a low-grade fever, which persisted for the next twenty years.

In 1973, after the severity of stomachaches increased, and I developed alternating constipation and diarrhea, I was hospitalized and diagnosed with an irritable colon. I switched doctors in 1974, to no avail. My stomachaches and other  symptoms were so severe and persistent that I took a three-month leave of absence from work.

By 1974, I was on my third doctor, Dr. Baxter, an internal medicine specialist. Again, more tests were run. Then he put me on

Bentyl and another medication. I took the medication and returned to work, but the stomach pain continued along with alternating constipation and diarrhea. My abdomen stayed physically sore, in addition to the stomachaches I experienced.

The fact I couldn't get an accurate diagnosis and treatment not only affected me physically, it plagued my mind. Why couldn't the doctors figure out what was wrong? I began to wonder if Steve and I would ever be able to start a family. If I got pregnant, would my body be able to endure the pregnancy? My level of function was already poor, and I had lost sixty pounds from a combination of dieting and staying sick

Much to my surprise, my worries were dispelled when I discovered I was pregnant in 1974. We had not planned it, but Steve and I were overjoyed. I stopped taking the other medication but continued taking the Bentyl. Morning sickness added to my overall feeling of not being well, though I was sick all the time—not just in the morning. On August 16, 1975, I delivered our son Matt after fifteen hours of labor. As we looked at Matt for the first time, Steve and I were thrilled with our perfect little boy. Matt was such a sweet and beautiful baby, and Steve beamed with pride that he had a son.

Almost immediately upon returning home from the hospital, postpartum depression set in. I wondered why my friends with new babies could go out and do things within a few weeks of giving birth. What was wrong with me? I felt bad, had no energy, and cried a lot. Steve never seemed to be home. He worked long hours and took classes at Clemson to prepare for an examination to receive his professional engineer's license.

Matt developed severe colic and cried all the time. I struggled to feed and burp him and then nurse him again. I slept very little, nor did I get much rest between feedings. Migraine headaches set in, which I'd never experienced before. My doctor recommended that I stop nursing Matt and switch to formula when he was four weeks old, so I did.

But the problems persisted. I got up five, six, or seven times a night, and Matt hardly slept at all during the day, either. Steve tried to get up some at night to help, but it was hard on him since he worked long hours. Sometimes Steve fell asleep on the couch, holding Matt, which scared me. I was so afraid Steve would drop him that I continued to get up as often as I was able.

The first time we ventured back to church with Matt was a disaster. During the service, the nursery worker didn't give Matt his colic medicine because she felt it wasn't good for him. Instead, she let him scream. When she finally gave in, it was too late and the medicine didn't help. I couldn't go back to church for a while after that. It upset me so bad to know my child could have been relieved of that pain and wasn't.

Steve felt I was overprotective of Matt. Our friends left their children in the nursery, sick or not, crying or not, so why couldn't I? Then the day came when I had to return to work. I visited day care facilities with Mother. None of them were suitable, not even the good ones. Disheartened, I returned home. How could I leave Matt when he cried all the time and hardly slept? I dreaded telling Steve, though I understood his worries of how we would make ends meet.

Steve's mother had worked his entire life at the Post Office and had to be at work by 6:00 a.m. each day. She then came home and cooked, cleaned house, and did all the things a mother and housewife should do. However, what I didn't realize at the time—and Steve didn't remember—was his family also had a woman who came in every day to help with the cleaning, child rearing, and cooking. Although Steve's mother worked hard, she didn't do nearly as much as Steve remembered she did or that he thought I should do, at least until Steve and his brothers were much older and didn't need anyone at home with them. I resented his lack of understanding and my own feelings of inadequacies. Why couldn't I just be normal like other women?

Being an extrovert, Steve wanted to go places and socialize with friends or have them over to our place to play cards, stay up late, and have fun. Between Matt and my health and sleep problems, this was another area of discord in our lives. Steve couldn't understand why our child wouldn't lie down at someone else's home and go right to sleep.

Even so, life happily continued on with our little family of three. We did fun things with our friends. On my good days, I'd have spurts of energy and work in the yard, sometimes washing and waxing the cars. I still loved to be outside, surrounded by nature. I had a beautiful vegetable garden. I savored those rare days.

In the early spring of 1976, we were surprised to discover I was pregnant again. Matt was eight months old. We had wanted three children, so although the news was unexpected, we were happy. However, I wasn't sure I could endure another pregnancy so soon, since I hadn't fully recovered from the first one. Matt still woke up several times every night. In spite of this, I knew this baby, too, was a gift from God. I was so excited and blessed to be carrying another child.

This second pregnancy was rougher than the first. I stayed sick, couldn't keep down food, and had severe stomach pains. When I thought our circumstances couldn't possibly get any worse, Steve came home with a surprise announcement.

The highway department wanted us to move to Bishopville, SC, a small town three hours southeast of Anderson. Steve would be promoted to maintenance engineer of Lee County, and Bishopville was the county seat. I should have been elated for my husband.

Under normal circumstances, I'm sure I would have been. Bishopville was so small, I'd never even heard of it. I could only think of how tiring the move would be, and I'd be giving up the only support system I had—my mother.

During this time, I had drawn closer to my mother than ever before. Compassion flowed from her when any of us were sick. She seemed to enjoy taking care of us.

In Anderson, we lived only two blocks from my parents. When Steve was at work, and I had a bad day, all I had to do was call Mother. She cooked lunch, if we needed it. She didn't like to babysit, but I went over to her house often and let her watch Matt while I grabbed a little uninterrupted sleep.

Though worried about the unknown, I was determined to be supportive and try to make the move work for Steve's sake. Steve and I drove to Bishopville to look for housing. We rode around for a while and couldn't even find a decent subdivision. Main Street was like stepping back into Mayberry—the town had such an old feel to it. The more we drove around finding nothing, the more upset I became. Tears began to run down my face. I wanted to go back home to Anderson and our friends, church, and family. After spending a short time checking out the small town of Bishopville, Steve agreed, and we headed back to I-20 for the three-hour drive home.

The next day, Steve told his boss he wouldn't take the promotion. His refusal wasn't taken well. To our dismay, the district engineer said another job was open in Goose Creek, South Carolina, which was even farther from Anderson. If we didn't take the Bishopville job, we would have to move to Goose Creek, if Steve wanted to continue working as an engineer for the highway department.

Neither Steve nor I were happy, but I decided if it must be, then I'd support my husband with a smile on my face. Maybe my first impression of Bishopville had been harsh. More importantly,

I'd vowed to be with Steve, for better or worse, no matter what. I would go anywhere to be with him. Yet I was plagued with doubts.

If only my child didn't have colic and slept better … If I didn't have such severe morning sickness from this pregnancy … If I hadn't been sick with "something" my entire life …

But what-ifs didn't count, and with me unable to work, this was our only option. Steve would receive a raise, manage an entire department, and supervise more than a hundred men. This was a first opportunity—an independent opportunity—for Steve to make his mark with the highway department.

Although there appeared to be only two options—join the unemployment line or move—I don't remember us praying together about the decision. As a matter of fact, Steve and I never prayed together. I had asked Steve a couple of times if we could, and he said of course, but he didn't bring it up later and neither did I. He was a substitute Sunday school teacher in our class and taught on a few occasions. I think that was the only time I heard him pray, except for the short blessings before we ate.

We had talked extensively during our courtship, but for some reason, after we got married, feelings, wants, desires, joys, and dreams weren't discussed anymore. Very early in our marriage, we reached a communication impasse.

Steve's mother said I needed to encourage and support my husband. He had worked hard to earn his engineering degree from Clemson. He should follow his dreams, and I should support that.

When I looked at her physical and mental strength, oh, how I wanted to be the kind of mother and wife she'd been and still was. Though I had silently accused Steve of comparing me to his mother, I did it too.

Determined to be strong and supportive, I thought I could will myself to be well.

I will trust in God, and He will help me. I love my husband and have been blessed with a beautiful little boy and another on the way. I will try harder to be the best wife and mother I can.

I kept telling myself these things. Somehow, I would succeed.

After making a couple more trips to Bishopville, Steve found an apartment he thought we could manage until we found something better. Late on a very hot August day, we left Anderson for Bishopville. Steve's mom went with us to help us get settled.

The landscape changed as we drove down the interstate. Trees were shorter and stumpy. The dirt was lighter, almost sandy, unlike the darker rich soil in Anderson. Steve smiled a lot to encourage me, so I tried my best to be happy.

When we arrived, I was hot, scared, and sick to my stomach. I also felt excitement. We were finally there. But my heart sank when we pulled up to the apartment, located in a poorer section of town. Its sliding glass doors opened onto the concrete parking lot. People constantly walked up and down the small street in front of our door. They were so close, they could see right into the sliding glass door, which let the only outside light into the den and kitchen.

The air conditioning didn't work. It must have been 110°F or more inside. Before the movers unloaded our furniture, Steve's mom noticed the carpet was dirty and had nails and pins imbedded in it. Steve had the movers unload our boxes into a hallway by our apartment door and the furniture into the parking lot. He finally found someone to clean the carpets, and by nightfall, we had moved in our beds. Steve's mother helped unpack some kitchen boxes.

That first day and night in Bishopville were probably the most miserable hours I'd ever spent in my life. It was hot, and Matt cried, so of course, we didn't sleep. We moved the furniture in the following day, and then Steve reported to work the day after.

Steve's mom stayed for a few days and helped me finish unpacking. She was helpful and kind, but again, admonished me to pull myself together for Steve's sake. In order for him to succeed, I needed to be a strong wife. I simply had to get over being sick and somehow manage with Matt and the new baby on the way.

Chapter Three

But God has surely listened and has heard my prayer.

PSALM 66:19

S teve was excited about his new position. I tried to be happy—I wanted to be happy and smile when he was around, but most of my days were spent in the dark apartment, crying often and afraid to open the curtains because of the people milling around outside.

Even the simplest activity like washing clothes was an ordeal. I had to roll the washer over to the sink and hook up the hoses to fill and then drain into the sink. Sometimes I let the clothes pile up in the small spare bathroom we used for a laundry closet. Once, I got so far behind, they grew mildew in that damp environment, and we had to throw them away as a result. I couldn't face the mountain of clothes and dragging the washing machine around the kitchen.

Shortly after moving, I developed a bladder infection and that's when I found a new OB/GYN. Her office was in Sumter, a thirty-minute drive from Bishopville. Knowing I had now found a good OB/GYN gave me peace of mind about this pregnancy.

In the midst of my depression and turmoil, an angel appeared in the form of an upstairs neighbor. I don't remember her name, but she and her husband temporarily lived in the apartment above us and had two small children. She quickly realized what a difficult time I was having and would come downstairs to check on me or talk, and sometimes I went up to her apartment. Her willingness to reach out to me was a lifeline. Mother called and checked on me almost every day, also.

We ventured out to church, First Baptist in Bishopville. At that time, many of the folks in Bishopville had grown up together, so fitting into the church felt as awkward as fitting into the community.

After a couple of months, Steve found a little modular home with three bedrooms and a bathroom on Main Street to rent. It even had a little den and screened-in porch. The kitchen was so small with no counter space, but we managed to fit a tiny table under a window. That's where I prepared meals. Walking into the bedrooms, we had to press our bodies against the wall to walk around our only heat source, a floor furnace. But we didn't care about the house's shortcomings. We were thrilled to be moving out of the dark and dreary apartment and into our new home.

I tried diligently to be "me" in our little house. I starched, ironed, and then hung cute café-style ruffled curtains at the windows. Neighbors dropped by saying they wanted to see who had moved into the neglected house and fixed it up to look so cute. I'd get bursts of energy where I'd feel well enough to tackle the yard work—cutting bushes and planting flowers. Despite the fact the work wore me out, these were things I loved to do. It was almost therapeutic for me. Steve arrived home each day to a neat and clean house with a delicious hot meal at lunch and at supper.

Our neighbors beside and across the street from us were older. We took the initiative and met our backdoor neighbors, the Atkinsons, a retired Methodist minister and his wife. They were nice to us, welcoming us into the town. I had someone to talk to and ask questions about the town, but it was mostly chit-chat. Since our house and backyard was on a corner, Steve fenced in the backyard so Matt could go out and play without my having to be with him every minute.

I am ashamed to say I don't really remember reading my Bible much at all during this stressful period. Most of the time, I was alone and didn't feel well, so it was a struggle to get through each day. That's when I should have turned to God (oh, how I needed Him), but I didn't.

We began attending First Baptist Church on a regular basis. We were welcomed more with each visit as we also got more involved. We joined a Sunday school class and started making good friends.

We planned events for the seniors and worked with the youth group in the church. Steve sang in the choir and sang solos. People gravitated to Steve's outgoing personality. I'd grown accustomed to this wherever we went.

I tried to put on a brave front and push myself physically beyond my strength, but I grew sicker. I lost weight, and my doctor became very concerned. She decided to induce labor early because of a cyst she'd detected on one of my ovaries. So Mother came down to stay with Matt.

As soon as I began the labor preparation at the hospital, I started having contractions. The labor room was large with many beds. There was no privacy like we had when Matt was born, and to my dismay, my labor and delivery had been very difficult with Matt, even with the pain medications I was given. We had also not been through Lamaze classes.

Although my doctor in Sumter was good, she also was a stern, hard woman, retired from the military. She would not hear of pain medications. She insisted I could do it alone. After chastising me, she said, "Oh, by the way, I sent your husband home. He didn't need to sit alone in the waiting room all night. Who knows when you'll have this baby?"

Terrified and alone, I was angry at her for saying that. I was even angrier at Steve for listening to her and leaving.

Right before leaving the room, she checked me and then exclaimed, "Oh my God, you're about to deliver right now."

This was before cell phones, so Steve was halfway back on a thirty-minute drive to Bishopville and couldn't be reached. As soon as he drove into the driveway, Mother sent him back to the hospital, but it was too late. I'd already delivered Andy. Labor and delivery had lasted fifteen hours just as it did with Matt.

The nurses brought Andy in to me, and Steve smiled broadly. He was so proud of his newborn son as was I. The nurse asked if I wanted to hold Andy. Oh yes, I did. He was so beautiful. The experience of giving birth all alone had left me scared, weak, and overwhelmed. This was such a special, memorable day, and I didn't have the energy to even hold my newborn son. Andy weighed over eight pounds, which was a big baby for me to deliver, especially with no meds. I looked at him with tears in my eyes as I thanked God he was so healthy and beautiful. I then had to ask to be taken to my room.

The nurses waited a little while and then brought Andy back in. Even though I still felt so bad, I was so anxious to see and hold my baby. I loved my little boy and cradled him in my arms, but I'd never felt so physically drained and in pain like I did at that moment.

Because of a flu epidemic in Bishopville, the hospital was closed to visitors. Steve's mother had come down. Mother wanted to see me, but the only one allowed in my room was Steve. Unfortunately, he worked all day.

I'd fix myself up each afternoon, put on makeup, and be smiling when Steve walked through the door each night. He talked on and on about how beautiful I looked, how beautiful Andy was, a perfect little boy. He'd stay for an hour or so and then have to leave. I'd cry myself to sleep after he left. I wouldn't let him see my bad emotional state. I didn't want to be depressed, so again, I thought I could will it away as long as no one else knew.

After I got out of the hospital, Mother went home, and Steve's mother stayed for a week to help. The tumor on my ovary grew, instead of shrinking as the doctor had hoped. On the bright side, Andy was such a good baby. As long as he was held, fed, and had a dry diaper, he'd go right back to sleep. We were still rocking Matt to sleep and getting up several times each night with him because of his colic. He was seventeen months old, and this should have cleared up by then. But I was blessed—so blessed with two beautiful sons.

I don't remember how soon I started back to church after Andy's birth. Steve kept going, getting more involved, going early and staying late sometimes. He also went on Wednesday night to choir practice. I didn't go anywhere unless we all went as a family, except maybe on a Saturday afternoon when Steve could stay with the boys. Then I went about two blocks from the house into downtown Bishopville for an hour or two.

In the midst of the transition we'd been through, I felt like I was losing me—I was losing Nancy. I felt worse after Andy was born. My muscles ached. Steve and I started to draw apart. Alone and sad, I needed my family. I needed my mother and sisters. I needed something, though at that time, I didn't know what. Now I know I needed God—and I needed Steve. Somehow I needed to find me again, to be whole and to live like everyone else around me did.

My mind was a blur. I couldn't figure out how to reach God. I must have been doing something wrong, I thought. To some extent, I was. Going to Sunday school and worship services every now and then isn't the same as really having a relationship with Him. Still, from time to time, I would mention again to Steve that it would be nice if we could pray together or have a devotional together. Every time, he would say, "Sure, that's a good idea." Then I would wait, and neither of us brought it up again.

When Andy was three months old, Steve took me back to Anderson to have the tumor on my ovary removed. Dr. Rice removed the ovary and cyst, which was the size of a grapefruit. I was in the hospital for a week, and then Steve had to return to Bishopville to work. The boys and I stayed at Mother's for a couple of weeks.

Steve missed me, which was nice because I already felt like such a burden. Since I couldn't pick up my babies, Steve hired a woman in Bishopville named Siss who'd taken care of many babies for the women of Bishopville over the years. She came and stayed with us. She couldn't read or write, but she took good care of the boys and obviously loved them. I would sometimes hear her singing to them and then calling them her "sweet babies." She cooked and cleaned and made life easier for me where she could. I eventually recovered enough from the surgery that Siss went home. It's strange that I still remember that particular day so well after so many years. I felt anxious and panicky, wondering if I could handle all the responsibilities of a young mother with two babies.

The months since we'd moved to Bishopville had been very stressful. Sicker than ever after the surgery, again, I questioned where God was in my life. His Word says He was with me, but I didn't feel it. Although I tried to pray, I didn't draw close to Him to receive everything I needed. Instead, I continued feeling alone, sick, and very sad.

We managed to muddle through two years in Bishopville. Steve excelled in his job, but we both missed Anderson, our family, and our way of life there. Then two unexpected things happened.

First, the highway department informed Steve they were transferring him to Columbia, the capital of South Carolina. Talk about going to extremes. Now we would have to adjust to a city several times larger than Anderson and go through the difficult process of moving again, this time with two small children.

Second, before the despair of this news set in, a miracle happened. Daddy called with news of a job opening for an engineer at Duke Power. This was the reprieve we'd hoped and prayed for—we were going home to Anderson. I was ecstatic!

God had heard my prayers. Although I failed to recognize it at the time, God had been with me during that awful time in Bishopville. Through it all, He knew our future.

Chapter Four

God did not allow His people to be oppressed so that they would be defeated, but so that they would ultimately be victorious.

BETH MOORE, *Breaking Free*

Soon after moving back to Anderson in 1978, we bought a spacious older home with a fenced-in backyard six blocks from my parents' house. Being around friends and family was incredible after two years of isolation in Bishopville.

Susan and Sandra still lived in Anderson, and neither was married. They doted on Andy and Matt. We'd never been particularly close growing up, mainly because they had each other. Now that I'd returned home, we became best friends. Susan came to me one day and said she realized what a difficult time I'd had being away from home with two small children and very little help. She offered to babysit Matt and Andy one day a week so I could get out and do something for myself. This continued for a number of weeks until Susan found a job. This new bond that developed between my sisters and me was really nice and made me feel I belonged.

Steve and I returned to Pope Drive Baptist Church. We slipped right back in with our friends. Soon Steve was there every time the doors opened. With Matt and Andy to get ready each week, I couldn't match Steve's dedication. As time progressed, it became more difficult for me to get up on Sunday morning and take both children to church. We began going separately, so Steve could go to Sunday school.

Steve joined the choir. He was elected deacon and served on more than one high-profile committee. He firmly believed if you were asked to do something within the church, it was the Lord's will, and you should do it. He went to church earlier and stayed later than the rest of us.

Staying home was easier for me because of the boys and my declining health. It was also nice that I could have a hot dinner prepared for Steve after church just as his mom and my mother had always done. When I attended church, I saw Steve from a distance in the church choir. Back then, Pope Drive didn't have a children's church, so when Matt turned three years old, he went to church with me. It was hard to keep a three-year-old quiet and occupied in church services. I didn't hear much of the sermon, and I was even more fatigued by the time church was over. As I stayed home more, Steve got more involved. The tension between us increased. He and I both knew I couldn't handle doing things other wives and mothers did.

Other people had babies and took them places, like the store or church, even after they had two or three children. I didn't understand. Why couldn't I do that too? I barely managed to do the grocery shopping, and then it was usually at night when I could go without the boys or as a family when Steve came home from work. I felt guilty, often telling myself I should take care of these things myself since my husband worked so hard. Not being able to take care of my home the way other women did was demoralizing. But Mother helped out as often as she could.

Steve and I made new friends at Pope Drive. We grew close to the choir director, Jimmy. He and his wife were our age. Their children were the same age as our boys. In 1979, Steve joined a singing group named Logia with three other men and two women, formed by Jimmy. They sang at different churches, sometimes at revivals and often at churches in other towns. Next they decided to embark on a summer tour. Since the other spouses planned to go, Steve wanted me to go.

I didn't think Mother would agree to keep Matt and Andy, who were two and three years old at the time. She complained that I didn't need to go—that neither of us should go. Parents should stay home to care for their families, she said.

I kept asking her, because Steve really wanted me to go. I'd been seeking and praying for the special intimacy we'd had early in our marriage to be rekindled. Knowing Steve wanted me to go along on the tour with him made me feel so special. We had not spent any time together alone since the birth of Matt and Andy.

Finally, Mother agreed to keep the boys, and all the other details of the tour fell into place.

As we left to go on this tour, I didn't feel strong, but I'd become good at hiding my pain, illness, and deep-rooted feelings of insecurity. I suppose some of it was my apprehension about the trip, which I didn't understand since Steve and I were so excited.

We took the church bus to Edgefield, South Carolina, where Logia sang before we went to Orlando, Florida. The group had a day off, so we spent it at Disney World. After Orlando, Logia sang in Deland, Florida. Next, we traveled to Cayce, South Carolina, then Camden, South Carolina, for appearances on the way home.

Steve's voice was strong and beautiful. He received many compliments. He has such an outgoing personality that he always talked to people after the concerts, graciously accepting praise for his solos. I was so proud of him, but I don't thrive in the spotlight like he does. I stood in the background watching and waiting for him. Occasionally, I walked up, or sometimes he called me over to introduce me to whoever he was talking with.

For the most part, we had a good time. If I had not felt weak during the trip, it would have been better. Steve and I enjoyed each other's company, and I could tell he was proud I was there with him, although the closeness we both longed for still wasn't there.

Even though we attended church, and Steve was involved in their singing ministry and served as a deacon, God was not at the center of our marriage, although Steve remembers that he felt closer to God then more than any other time. We went to church and put on a good act, as many people do, but God wasn't paramount in our lives.

The sense of renewal I felt after the bus tour was short-lived. We had not recaptured the intimacy in our marriage like I'd hoped. I assumed responsibility and decided if I looked better, maybe that would help. Although I had not gained much weight during my pregnancies, I didn't exercise and was overweight. I reasoned that if I exercised, I'd feel and look better and Steve would love me more.

I bought some leotards and tights—and joined a gym. I went three nights a week when Steve could stay with the boys. I began to feel a little stronger, so I tried jogging a little as well. This turned out not to be a good idea since I could only run slowly for about a half block before I had to stop.

I came home from the gym in my little black outfit, excited by the new exercises I'd learned, and tried to show them to Steve. Maybe he'd be proud of me for making the effort, for losing some weight, and getting more limber. Maybe he would be more attracted to me, maybe this would make us closer, but it didn't.

Steve still came home for lunch because he worked five minutes away. In addition to cooking a full meal at lunch, I'd cook breakfast and dinner. I didn't realize how incredibly unhealthy this was for us. I baked a cake once a week. I wanted to be a good homemaker like other women, especially Steve's mom and my mother. Our diet consisted of dishes like chicken and dumplings, fried chicken, rice and gravy and of course, a few veggies seasoned with bacon. All the fattening Southern food. I'd make cobbler or pies to go with it. No wonder I wasn't losing much weight—and feeling so horrible.

Then a friend told me about a grapefruit diet. On this diet, you'd eat half of a grapefruit before each meal, and then at each meal you ate specific things. I normally didn't eat grapefruit or even drink orange juice because they hurt my stomach, but I was determined not to quit once I started it.

In my desperation to become the woman I believed my husband wanted, whoever or whatever that was, I followed the diet despite the ill effects to my health. The more I dieted, the worse my stomach hurt. It was a vicious cycle of trying to make myself more attractive and feel better, yet none of my efforts worked. Steve and I grew further and further apart.

It's difficult when your husband is so involved at church because you think maybe that's what God wants him to do. From my vantage point, it seemed Steve was more interested in being around other people, being at church every time the doors opened and being at the center of many activities. It wasn't until years later that Steve confided in me that many a Sunday he looked around at the other families worshiping together and he really missed seeing his own family. How ironic, that is what we both desired all along.

Yet how could I compete? Why should I *try* to compete with that? I prayed a lot about my feelings that the church was taking Steve away from me.

Financially, we struggled. We lived off one salary and had just bought our first house. As a stay-at-home mom, I watched every penny we spent. I couponed, which was more difficult and time consuming than couponing today. I saved UPC codes from packages and grocery receipts. Often, ads ran in the newspaper or magazines where if you sent in three UPC codes from a particular box of cereal along with the cash register receipt, you'd get two dollars off that cereal. I had a three-drawer file cabinet in my little office to keep the coupons categorized.

One day, I had a long grocery list and massive amounts of coupons. I had so many coupons, some items I could get for free. It took much planning to organize the list and coupons into the proper size and product amounts.

Overwhelmed by the thought of taking a three-year-old and almost five-year-old to the store, I called Mother to see if she wanted to go with me. I didn't always call her to go, but that day I felt strange. I needed to buy groceries. Staying home wasn't an option. Mother also needed some items, so she agreed to go.

We each had a boy in our cart. That day, the store brimmed with shoppers due to double coupons. With my cart loaded, I got in a long line to pay. Already stressed from shopping, the longer I stood there, the more anxious I became. Mother was in line next to me and got to the checkout before I did in my line.

My pulse raced, and my heart began to pound hard in my throat. My vision blurred, and I thought I might pass out. The closer I got to the checkout counter, I started running scenarios through my head.

Am I going to stay and go through the ordeal of taking the time to use my coupons or pick up my children and leave?

The latter wasn't a viable option. I'd already done all the work, and we needed the groceries. So I stayed in line. When it was my turn, I put the groceries on the counter. My hands and arms shook. I felt weaker as my heart pounded harder and faster.

While Mother completed her checkout, I asked the cashier to get me a chair because I felt lightheaded. She called her manager. I didn't want to draw attention to myself, with so many people around, but I couldn't make myself leave.

The manager brought a chair, and then Mother came over and asked, "What's the matter?"

"I don't know." I sat in the chair with head leaned over to keep from passing out. My blood pressure was probably high, along with my heart rate. Something terrifying was happening in my body.

Finally, the cashier finished checking my groceries. Mother took my checkbook, wrote a check, and helped us to my car while the bagboy loaded our groceries. Mother drove us back to my house. My pulse quieted, but I felt like my body had been through something catastrophic. I barely had the strength to walk into the house and lie on the couch. Mother took care of the boys, unloaded my groceries, and put my refrigerated items away. She put her cold items in my fridge, and then called Steve.

Dazed, crying, and exhausted, I just wanted Andy and Matt not to be so loud.

Steve rushed home. When he came into the living room, he smiled. Kind and concerned, he wanted to know if I was okay.

"What's going on?"

"I don't know what's going on." I knew Mother had already filled him in on what had transpired in the grocery store, and I didn't have the strength to rehash it.

"That's okay," he said, "You'll be all right. I'll run your mother home, and I'll be right back."

When Steve returned, he put away the remaining groceries, took care of Matt and Andy, and fixed supper. I could get up to go to the bathroom but had no strength for anything else. He brought my supper to me that night. I had no idea what was happening. I kept saying maybe I have a virus. I became dizzy and lightheaded when I tried to stand, though I wasn't nauseated or feverish. Steve took off the next day from work because I couldn't take care of the boys.

Several days went by that I wasn't left at home alone with kids or by myself because I felt so bad. Mother took me to our family doctor, Dr. Baxter, considered one of the best doctors in Anderson at the time. He did a physical and said it was nothing to worry about—I had "housewife syndrome."

Housewife syndrome? What's that? Are you just saying that because you don't know what's wrong with me?

He talked about what stress could do to my body and how my anxiety could make my body feel like it was running away uncontrolled. He said I needed something to calm my anxiety. He gave me an antidepressant or an antianxiety medicine. I went home and took the medicine. About an hour later, weird sensations started running up the back of my neck into my head—like fireworks exploding in my head. They would come in waves, one explosion and then another. Every time, I'd have to hold onto something to keep from falling.

I called the doctor and spoke with the nurse. The doctor called me in a different medication. Over the course of the next few weeks and months, I tried several medications, though I don't remember what they were. None worked. I had become extremely sensitive to anything and everything I put in my mouth.

I know now, in addition to the medication sensitivities, our house was not environmentally friendly. The gas heat bothered me. Smells and leaks permeated the house. Several years later, I learned how allergic I am and how my body reacts dramatically to smells, the environment, and to any medicine. I'd been that way for years, to some degree, but didn't realize it, before the attack.

After the attack, every such reaction grew substantially more severe. The weeks and months that followed are a blur in my memory as I now think back trying to piece them together. I don't remember much about this time, except that I lay on the couch or in a bed most of the time. Mother came over and stayed with me on weekdays. Sometimes, Steve's mother drove from Iva and stayed. I'd get up to eat or go to the bathroom. My heart pounded so hard in my throat, I could count heartbeats. I was afraid—terribly afraid—to be left alone at all.

I'd wake up in middle of night with scared, panicked feelings. Steve held me, and I cried because I felt so bad. This went on for months.

In the midst of this horror, when I couldn't see God at work in my life, He was. God blessed me with the tenacity to fight for what I know is right—part of which was trying to get a proper diagnosis. I knew my ailment was biological in nature. My God-given intuition led me to make good choices, even when those around me doubted.

When my body couldn't tolerate the psychotropic medications, I had to stand up and say, "Enough!" My loved ones and doctors scoffed at my choices, because they believed my illness was in my mind.

Today, we have the Internet to do medical research. No one had heard of the Internet back then. In fact, no one had computers in their homes. All I could do was go from doctor to doctor in search of answers.

My family wanted me to be well, but no one was proactive in helping me get there. This led me to believe they thought of this as a choice I needed to make rather than an illness that needed a cure. Sure, my mother or Steve would take me to any doctor I wanted to see, but they didn't understand why I didn't take every medicine prescribed, no matter the side effects. I didn't feel the support, encouragement, and active participation I desperately needed from them as I struggled to figure out what I could and couldn't take. I felt the difference daily from those closest to me.

Friends and family lost patience. I resented their attitude, but at the same time, I couldn't really blame them. How could I expect them to understand what the best doctors in town couldn't understand— what I couldn't understand myself? And I was the one living it. I began to give up and think perhaps death would be better than living like this. I prayed God would take me to end my suffering.

I realize my friends honestly didn't know what to do. They wanted to help, but if they dropped by, and I was lying on the couch, unable to show the Southern hospitality others could with guests, it created an awkward atmosphere.

One day during this first acute illness, an old friend dropped by. She didn't call, so we didn't know she was coming. I was on the couch, which had pretty much become my spot. Of course, she was nice and friendly and asked what was wrong.

"Well, I think I must have a virus I can't get over." I didn't know what else to say. I do remember my heart pounded hard in my chest when I heard her walk up to our front door. My adrenalin flowed, like it did in the store. I couldn't figure out why I felt anxious.

She stayed for a while, talking and smiling. We talked about Matt and Andy, because she didn't have any children yet. She talked about her husband, their vacations, and the new house they were building. So many things she discussed made Steve and I both envious and sad.

She meant well and tried to cheer me up. Cheer me up from what? She didn't know, and I didn't know. What a really strange situation!

Relief swept over me when she left, which made me feel guilty and even sadder. I could hardly walk to the bathroom, and my friend bubbled with energy.

She called a few times during the next few weeks, but she didn't come back. Her calls decreased as she would always ask what was wrong, and I didn't have an answer. She gradually began to talk to Steve more than me on the phone. But, he didn't know what to say either. It was difficult on him, being a man who wanted to be able to fix things. How could he fix something he didn't understand?

Another close friend's husband, who had a background in mental health care, called Steve after I had been sick for a month or two with no change. Steve took the phone into the bedroom, but I could still hear his end of the conversation. The gist of the conversation was, if any hope existed in my improving, I needed to be put in an institution to deal with my emotional problems. Well, thank goodness Steve didn't listen to him. I think he considered it, though, before deciding we would try other avenues first.

Even though I felt discouraged we didn't know the cause of my illness, I believed I would get better soon! One day I'd wake up, and this nightmare would be over. I clung to this hope like a lifeline.

I tried so often to pray. But my prayers, which started out as weak, breathy pleas for relief, changed over time. When you pray and read the Bible often enough without one scintilla of evidence you've been heard by God, your prayers change.

For a while, my talks with God were bargaining sessions, whereby I promised to be a better wife and mother, promised to be a stronger Christian, if God would only take away this "thing" ravaging my body.

Then, at times, my prayers resembled more of a shouting match with my God, who seemingly refused to be my Savior and my constant friend. I desperately wanted and needed him to be both.

I'd always felt more fragile and weaker than my friends. I was an expert at hiding what went on inside my body. People would think less of me if they knew some dark, secret, nameless "thing" inside me—this "thing" that now made me and others question my mental stability.

The biggest hurt of all was Steve doubted me.

I know he suffered, also, and was as bewildered as I was that I couldn't get well. But his focus seemed to be on our plans and dreams we'd talked about before we were married that now were going unfulfilled. He hung his hopes on the medical profession and took me to numerous doctors in search of a cure. But if we'd worked together, maybe we would've been able to arrive at a diagnosis sooner. Hindsight is perfect, and "if onlys" don't count.

Instead, my undiagnosed illness created a deeper chasm between us. Little did I realize that this chasm would become an even deeper pit before God's revelation of His wondrous plans for our lives.

Chapter Five

The Lord Himself goes before you and will be with you;
He will never leave you nor forsake you.
Do not be afraid; do not be discouraged.

DEUTERONOMY 31:8

At twenty-nine years old, not knowing how my body would feel when I awakened each day depressed me. Would I be able to do anything worthwhile? Would an anxiety attack return at any moment to wreck yet another day?

Would I be able to drive my children to fun activities or run errands? Could I attend tonight's volleyball game to cheer on my husband? I longed to accomplish the simple tasks everyone else took for granted. Weeks after I had the anxiety attack, I was even more fearful of its return.

Discouraged because I had been sick for several weeks, I tried to reassure myself this couldn't last much longer, but how could I?

Although I'd had stomach problems most of my life, I still considered myself a strong, physically active person. Sure, I had setbacks through my pregnancies and surgery, but I had eventually rebounded. I did yard work and planted a garden. Not long before the spell in the grocery store, I'd been exercising.

Hopefully this is all temporary. Steve and I can have a wonderful, fulfilling life; I just have to figure out a way to get back what we've lost. I know if I try hard enough, I can do it.

We enjoyed our boys so much as we looked forward to them being Boy Scouts one day, because Steve had been active in Boy Scouts, as I was in Girl Scouts. We anticipated Little League and music lessons. Our families had taken vacations to the beach at least once every summer, so we wanted our sons to experience the same fun trips we had experienced.

I loved the mountains and envisioned us climbing up mountain trails looking for snakes, bugs, and all the critters little boys love. Picnics in the park, football games, baseball games, and so much more were in our hopes and dreams for our family.

Oh, how I wanted to be a good mother and do all sorts of fun things with my boys. I wanted to play softball or kickball in the backyard with them like Mother did on a few occasions when she felt better. I wanted to teach them how to swim and take them to a pool in the summer.

Steve and I had dreams of this perfect family life. I had so many dreams that I could never, ever begin to count them all. I wanted it all—Steve wanted it all.

In spite of the health problems looming in the background my entire life, I had always been filled with determination and figured out a way to do anything I wanted to do.

I once took apart our huge couch and reupholstered it when Steve left on a week-long business trip. I'd never done anything like that before. We couldn't afford to pay to get the couch covered and it needed a bit of TLC, so I saved the money, used inexpensive fabric, and recovered it myself. The house overflowed with strings, material, and stuffing when he returned home, but I was so proud.

I painted the inside of our house. I washed the windows, inside and outside. Neighbors would walk into our home and be awed by the starched, crisp ironed curtains with the pretty ruffles. I had arrangements of fresh flowers. They weren't really flowers most of the time but weeds from a nearby field which I arranged in such a way that they still looked pretty.

When we didn't have the money to buy the nice things I wanted, I made them or figured out an inexpensive way to make ours look as pretty as store bought. At Christmas, we still use beautiful ornaments of Santas, Christmas trees, snowmen, and Christmas bells I made from dough, which were painted perfectly. They rivaled high-priced store-bought ornaments.

We had old furniture mostly, but I took the time to sand, stain, and paint each piece, making them look pretty. I had Mother's old furniture, and I cherished my grandmother's old furniture. I made having so little look beautiful; we appeared to have many material blessings.

So why couldn't I function now? Why couldn't I will myself to overcome this illness that had a merciless grip on me?

My extended family had their lives. Neither they nor Steve could babysit me and the boys forever.

I prayed every day: *Lord, please help me. What's going on with me?*

Steve started to question me. "If this is a virus, you should be feeling better. What's 'housewife syndrome'?" He missed a lot of work caring for me. I knew it had to be hard on him.

One day, I thought, *This is crazy. I was exercising a few weeks ago and felt strong.*

That must be the answer! I needed exercise to build up my body. Exercise had improved my health before. I didn't want anybody to see me in my physical condition, so I went into the backyard and walked the periphery for fifteen to twenty minutes. As I walked, my lower back started to cramp and tighten. That had never happened before. I thought if I walked faster, got stronger, my symptoms would improve. By the time I stopped and went inside, the muscle spasms were severe in my lower back, hips, and legs.

Reflecting back, the grocery store incident and the exercise-induced muscle spasms were probably the beginning of full-blown fibromyalgia. I'd had other symptoms before with irritable bowel syndrome and some minor muscle spasms in my arms and neck during my pregnancy when I tried to shop, but this was different.

Even before then, during trips to my in-laws' garden, I had bouts of weakness and muscle spasms. Steve's mom showed me how to freeze and can the apples, pears, or sweet potatoes we got from their garden. I don't know how old she was then, but she was almost thirty years older than me. She could stand with a knife in her hand and peel fruit for hours. I couldn't. After I peeled only two or three, my hands, forearms, arms, and shoulder would become weakened and tremble. This is another time I noticed muscle problems.

But that day after walking in the backyard, not only was I severely anxious, I had muscle spasms daily. When I stood, I felt weak, dizzy, and shaky—all the virus symptoms I already had, but now my lower back and trunk were weak too.

I got up each morning and tried to sit on the couch. I sat on bed pillows because my sciatic nerves running down both legs and hips were so painful, I could hardly sit on any piece of furniture in the house. Even then, my legs hurt and tingled, got numb, and then I'd have to lie back down in bed. I couldn't walk around much because my muscles wouldn't support me.

I tried repeatedly to analyze my illness; that's all I had to do with my time. Had I missed something? Was I not the person God wanted me to be? Was I not a good enough wife, mother, daughter, and Christian? Why would He let this happen to me? I had already endured many struggles in my life since I was a little girl. Must I bear more? What could I do to get better?

Why? Why? Why?

My mind and heart exploded with questions, hurt, and self-doubt. The pain was unbearable at times. My muscles felt like big mooring ropes people use to tie boats up at a dock—knotty, thick, and cumbersome. Even sitting on pillows only worked temporarily—long enough to eat a meal and then go back to bed.

My typical day consisted of getting up and eating breakfast. I slipped on a soft pair of pants and a top without a bra. (I couldn't wear a bra for over fifteen years because it hurt so much.) Then, after a little while, I went back to bed. I didn't sleep all the time. As a matter of fact, I lay awake most of the time, praying and thinking about what my life had become. Sometimes whoever was at the house with me came in, sat a while, and talked, in an effort to cheer me up.

Midday, I got up and ate lunch, sometimes able to sit for a while before returning to bed. I despised this awful existence! I couldn't spend the rest of my life like this. When I wasn't thinking about suicide (which really wasn't as often as most might think), I tried to figure out the solution to my problems.

How could I feel better? Was there a book I could buy? A doctor I hadn't seen yet?

I wanted to scream, *Can anybody help me?*

I felt so isolated. Our pastor had quit calling. People at church had mostly stopped asking Steve about me. He didn't know what to say. How could I blame him? I'm sure he felt relieved when they stopped inquiring.

What could he say?

Well, no, she is about the same ... No, we don't know exactly what is wrong ... She is very weak ... She won't leave the house ... It upsets her to be out in public … We have had to rush her to the emergency room on several occasions because her blood pressure became dangerously high … Yes, we have been to many doctors … No, they still don't know what to do … No, I don't think she would enjoy company right now.

Questions, questions, questions … embarrassment … pain …. no answers … none!

The questions were hard on Steve. On Sundays, before he and the boys would leave for church, I'd ask him to request prayer for me. He would get a sad, questioning look in his eyes, and say, "Okay, I will if I get a chance."

When he returned home, I would ask if they had prayed for me. Sometimes Steve said yes. Other times, he said he hadn't gotten a chance to ask.

We rarely had visitors, but I had gotten to the point when people did visit, my heart pounded so hard and loud I was sure everyone could hear it. Relief swept through me when they finally left.

Steve couldn't continue to take time off work to care for me. When Mother and Daddy were able, the boys and I went to their house. Steve got Matt and Andy dressed and fed in the mornings, I managed to get clothes on, and Steve dropped us off at my parents' house on his way to work.

Daddy was sick at the same time. He'd retired but had Parkinson's, peripheral neuropathy, heart problems, and other health issues to deal with. He spent most of the time in my old bedroom (the former den in the middle of the house). Mother stayed in their bedroom. The kitchen was next to his room, so when he was in bed, she could check on him, and they could talk back and forth between the kitchen and bedroom. She hadn't worked outside the home since before my sisters and I were born.

Mother wasn't used to taking care of two little ones again. She tried to have patience, but caring for toddlers upset her. But, strangely, the way mother treated me then was the best she'd ever treated me. It seemed like the sicker I became, the more love and concern I received from her, which was odd because that's what I needed for so many years. She was the only one who didn't judge me or say, *You just have to stop this. You just have to get up and force yourself to be well.*

Since my mother cooked their big meal of the day at noon, Steve joined us for lunch. I was in such tremendous pain, I didn't realize how incredibly difficult this situation must have been on Mother.

Steve tried as best he could to work, then come home and do what he needed to do at home, taking care of me and the boys. Matt started playschool in the fall. Steve took him to school, or he'd go to work first then come home and take him or Mother would take Matt to preschool. Some days I managed at home with Andy. Other days Steve took us to Mother's.

I wasn't incapable of making decisions, but my reasoning was affected because so many people didn't believe I was physically sick. They thought it was in my head. Way too many conversations went on inside our home and on the telephone where Steve and other loved ones talked in whispered tones.

Friends and family discussed my panic attacks. Only, they weren't very good at being secretive. Among the remarks I overheard were, "I can't believe someone would get so scared they wouldn't want to leave their home," or "Why can't she just get in her car, trust God to get her where she needs to go, and quit putting so much pressure on her sweet, overworked husband?"

One more thing I learned about what people think about certain illnesses. No one believed panic attacks were real but something you can control and make up your mind to get over.

I still saw Dr. Baxter, but I started going to other doctors, as well. Steve and I made several trips to the emergency room, where I received the same irritable bowel syndrome (IBS) or other anxiety-related diagnoses.

As time went by, my anxiety only worsened. One night, I felt like I was going to crawl out of my skin. I couldn't tolerate sound at all. I called Mother and asked if she'd come get the boys and take them to her house to spend the night. Mother was hospitable up to the point of caring for Matt and Andy on her own. She didn't want them to ever spend the night. I must have sounded desperate because she came and got them.

It was winter, and Steve had started a fire in the fireplace. I lay on the couch in our den. Steve turned on the television, and I couldn't stand the sound, so I asked him to turn it off.

Scared, I prayed.

God I don't know what's happening to me. God, please help me. If there's anything you want me to learn, please tell me what it is. Please show me what it is.

Many times a day, I was now reading and jotting down notes in my Bible as I prayed for God to lead me to His answer.

Please show me, please tell me, please lead me to the verses that tell me what you want me to learn and I will learn it. If I've done anything

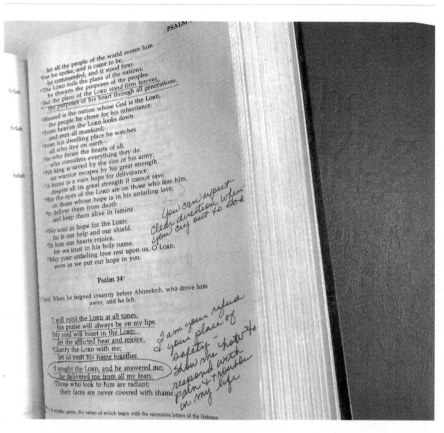

¹³I am still confident of this:
   I will see the goodness of the LORD
   in the land of the living.
¹⁴Wait for the LORD;
   be strong and take heart
   and wait for the LORD. *I am waiting*

Psalm 28

Of David.

¹To you I call, O LORD my Rock;
   do not turn a deaf ear to me.
For if you remain silent,
   I will be like those who have gone down to the pit.
²Hear my cry for mercy
   as I call to you for help, *Cry out with*
as I lift up my hands *your VOICE*
   toward your Most Holy Place.

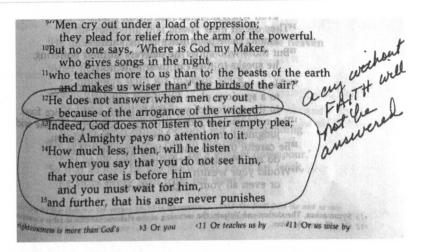

⁹"Men cry out under a load of oppression;
    they plead for relief from the arm of the powerful.
¹⁰But no one says, 'Where is God my Maker,
    who gives songs in the night,
¹¹who teaches more to us than to° the beasts of the earth
    and makes us wiser than° the birds of the air?'
¹²He does not answer when men cry out
    because of the arrogance of the wicked.
¹³Indeed, God does not listen to their empty plea;
    the Almighty pays no attention to it.
¹⁴How much less, then, will he listen
    when you say that you do not see him,
    that your case is before him
    and you must wait for him,
¹⁵and further, that his anger never punishes

a cry without FAITH will not be answered

righteousness is more than God's   ᵇ3 Or you   ᶜ11 Or teaches us by   ᵈ11 Or us wise by

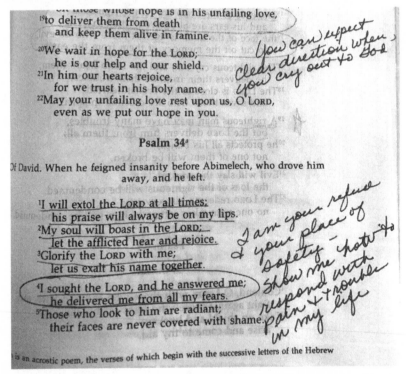

...those whose hope is in his unfailing love,
¹⁹to deliver them from death
    and keep them alive in famine.
²⁰We wait in hope for the LORD;
    he is our help and our shield.
²¹In him our hearts rejoice,
    for we trust in his holy name.
²²May your unfailing love rest upon us, O LORD,
    even as we put our hope in you.

You can expect Clear direction when you cry out to God

Psalm 34ᵃ

Of David. When he feigned insanity before Abimelech, who drove him
away, and he left.

¹I will extol the LORD at all times;
    his praise will always be on my lips.
²My soul will boast in the LORD;
    let the afflicted hear and rejoice.
³Glorify the LORD with me;
    let us exalt his name together.
⁴I sought the LORD, and he answered me;
    he delivered me from all my fears.
⁵Those who look to him are radiant;
    their faces are never covered with shame.

I am your refuge & your place of safety - show me how to respond with pain & trouble in my life

ᵃ is an acrostic poem, the verses of which begin with the successive letters of the Hebrew

wrong, please point it out to me so I can ask you for forgiveness and begin to correct it.

Terrified, I couldn't cry too hard because I feared the ramifications on my body. But on the inside, I screamed for help. Steve sat on the floor beside the couch that night and propped his elbow and arm up on the couch where I could hold his hand.

He had started the fire, thinking I would enjoy the coziness and warmth. The nice sound of a fire burning is supposed to be calming and peaceful; I have always loved one. Every crackle of the fire was like another explosion in the back of my head. My body actually jumped every time the fire cracked. Steve had to extinguish the fire.

This was one of many episodes of sights, sounds, or odors in my environment attacking my body. All of my senses seemed to be on hyper alert at all times. Startled by the smallest things, I then had to wait for thirty minutes to an hour for my body to calm down.

My doctor hadn't helped me. He'd suggested my problem was psychological and encouraged my family to believe it. Each doctor we went to ran tests and then said the same thing. Steve tried to be supportive in his own way, but he was muddling through uncharted territory the same as I. He was a young man with a beautiful family and ready to get on with life. I can't blame him that he waffled between patience and frustration.

After all, why couldn't I just *be* well?

Steve often took me to the hospital to have tests done on my colon or stomach. By that time, the muscles had gotten so bad from my back to my hips and legs, I couldn't wear shoes anymore. I wore a flat pair of old bedroom shoes. I'd worn them so much the little bit of padding in the bottom had deteriorated and one had a hole on its side, but that's all I could tolerate on my feet.

So when I had to go to the doctor or hospital, I wore baggy clothes because clothes hurt my body and skin, and I wore those raggedy bedroom shoes. I gained all the weight back I'd lost by virtue of spending most of my days in bed or on the couch. Leaving my house was embarrassing. I didn't have the energy to put on much makeup or fix my hair. Steve was always clean shaven, his hair groomed, and dressed nicely. I felt fat and ugly standing beside him.

My tests came back negative—as always. The doctors would look at me and say, "Nothing's wrong. Your blood work is fine. You probably just have IBS or low blood sugar."

Even as my health deteriorated, Steve still attended church as much as he could. He took the boys some. He'd leave early for choir practice and then Sunday school, so he didn't always take them.

When questioned about where I was, Steve started telling people I had panic attacks and couldn't stand being in crowds or around people. That was true, but it wasn't the whole truth.

During this time, my doctors tried a series of medications, probably ten to fifteen in all. Yet none of them worked. On my worst days, I languished in a hellish nightmare with no end. On the even rarer days when I felt better, I yearned for a solution. I couldn't go on like this forever.

You hear of people hitting rock bottom and then some precipitating event starts their climb back up. I thought I'd long since hit bottom while spending more than a year trapped in this miserable debilitated state, but I hadn't even come close. One morning my health took a decided turn for the worse.

Chapter Six

I can do all things through Christ who strengthens me.

PHILIPPIANS 4:13 NKJV

Like every other day, Steve went to work that morning. And like every other day, I lay on the couch feeling miserable—this day more so than usual. My heart pounded so hard, my veins pulsated in my wrist.

Short of breath and terrified, I called Mother. She rushed over. I could hardly speak to tell her I needed to go to the hospital. I feared I was dying or having a heart attack. She called Steve and he immediately came home. As my condition worsened, they discussed what to do.

Inside, I screamed for help, but again, I couldn't give voice to what was happening. I might have a heart attack. I might die. I might die. I couldn't let myself get more worked up. I finally whispered, "I have to go to the emergency room."

Steve said, "Let's not rush things."

I kept whispering that I had to go.

He finally agreed. He and Mother held onto me and walked me to the car. Somehow, they got me inside the backseat. My body collapsed as I fell over, unable to sit up.

When Mother and Steve pushed me into the ER in a wheelchair, a nurse and doctor walked over, and she tried to get me to do paperwork.

"Help me," I whispered. "I'm dying."

She felt my pulse, and then she and the doctor immediately rushed me to a room.

My blood pressure was 212/130, and my pulse was 168. The doctor ordered an injection of Vistaril and kept checking my blood pressure and pulse. Then they gave me a second shot.

Steve finally realized the gravity of the situation. He called our pastor. The hospital staff had jerked my shirt off to do an EKG, and I didn't even have the strength to cover myself when our pastor arrived.

After the second shot of Vistaril, my body began to calm down. Our pastor prayed with us before I was admitted to the hospital. I lay in bed sedated and very weak, but my heart didn't race anymore.

Steve stayed with me that day and the next, but then he had to return to work. Mother kept the boys. The hospital didn't run tests. They just kept me on bed rest and continued the Vistaril, now in pill form, eight per day.

Steve visited during his lunch break. He helped me up and walked me to the nurse's desk and then back to bed. That's all the energy I had. He came in the evenings after work and walked with me again. We walked a little farther each time. One day, I heard a nurse say, "What in the world is wrong with that woman, anyway? Why is she here?"

Feeling isolated, I thought, *Maybe everyone is right. Maybe I'm losing my mind. Maybe they will put me away.* Then I'd think, *No, that's not right. I'm really sick.*

I was discharged and went home with a prescription of Vistaril and took six to eight pills a day. Although the medicine calmed my anxious state, it did little for my overall health. In fact, I got weaker and more lethargic.

Life returned to the routine we had before the hospitalization. Somehow I managed each morning with Andy while Matt was in school. Some mornings Steve took me to Mother's, and she helped me with Andy and then with both boys through the summer.

Matt started to first grade that year. I muddled through the fall, and the holidays approached. At Christmas, my side of the family came over on Christmas Eve, and Steve's side of the family came the day before Christmas Eve. That had become our family tradition, which neither of us wanted to stop.

Christmas Day was for our little family to celebrate. Sometimes Mother and Daddy or my sisters would stop by for a visit. Steve wanted to continue our traditions, but I couldn't cook, clean, or decorate. Steve did everything as I lay on the couch, even as I opened presents.

Steve worked diligently at home and not only during the holidays, but the strain of having to compensate for my inability to help continued between us.

My mother had never been supportive of seeing a doctor for mental health issues. She'd always thought counselors and psychiatrists were for weak people, certainly not anybody in our family. I'm sure on some level she related to my illness because she had always been sickly. But my level of function wasn't as good as hers. I guess she began to believe at least part of my problem was psychological and I needed help with that part. So when she suggested I see a counselor, I began to reassess the severity of my condition.

I've had a broken self-image my entire life. I never quite felt good enough, actually more like a failure. So, when I became debilitated, I became more depressed and down on myself. Once again, I was such a huge failure, not only as a wife, but a mother too.

Somehow in my frazzled, foggy mind, I grasped something had to change. Although I had contemplated suicide, it wasn't an option. My faith in God overrode my desire to die. I clung to the hope a solution existed ... somehow, somewhere, sometime. Since no doctor, family member, or friend had been able to help me find that solution, it was up to me to figure it out. The first step was to try to regain some of my independence and self-worth.

But a counselor? We didn't have money for that. We had a mortgage payment, two little boys to support, and I couldn't work. Mother called a therapist who rented a house in my parents' neighborhood while building their new house.

Dr. Anderson agreed to see me for a very reasonable fee. He used an office in the former boys' home in Anderson to see patients at night. I wouldn't have to go through the county mental health center to see him, as I would if I saw him during the day.

It was nerve wracking to seek this kind of help—telling someone about my life and reliving the nightmare of it all with essentially a complete stranger.

Steve, however, thought it was a good idea. He drove me to the appointments because I didn't have a driver's license anymore. I had let it expire because my panic attacks were so bad I couldn't drive.

When we arrived for the first appointment and I saw the distance from the parking lot to the door, the short walk seemed almost insurmountable in my weakened state. Steve held onto me as we walked up the long walkway. I wore the same bedroom shoes I'd worn for years because I still couldn't wear shoes. The few steps leading into the building I climbed slowly. I thought I would never get in the door. Once inside, I tried all three chairs in the waiting room before finding one I could sit in without being in so much pain.

I wouldn't let Steve leave, so he and the boys sat in the car while I went in for the appointment. I was probably there an hour to an hour and a half. Dr. Anderson talked about different aspects of my life and asked many questions.

He said I was having panic attacks. He never indicated there could be anything physically wrong. He focused on my anxiety, really listened when I talked, and encouraged me.

I remember after one visit, I thought it was strange because, after talking with him and getting my feelings out, I felt a little stronger. The next time, he wanted Steve to come in with me, so Mother kept the boys.

Steve didn't feel he had any problems that needed to be discussed. Whatever was wrong was my problem. So that visit didn't go well.

After that, Steve continued to drive me and sat in the car with the boys during the appointment, but he refused to go in. This added to my guilt, but I'd finally found a lifeline, one I wouldn't walk away from.

Dr. Anderson and I talked about my other doctors and the drugs they prescribed. He seemed to understand why I couldn't take most of them. He made me feel like I was a normal person thinking clearly, and not a failure, or someone with a mental problem, when I said I couldn't take a certain medication.

Steve still didn't understand when I couldn't take medications because he thought each prescription would be the answer to my becoming happy and healthy again. I do understand that he wanted that so badly, because I did too. No matter how hard I tried to explain, I couldn't get him to understand my ordeal and that I needed help from the right people.

Part of the problem, though, was that I didn't understand my illness, nor did I have a clue as to who could help me. So much stress existed between us in our marriage because of the unknowns and our different ways of interpreting my illness. We were both victims in different ways.

Each counseling session gave me strength to face the next week. I was still very sick and in pain, but my stress level and depression had lightened. Dr. Anderson seemed to understand what I was going through and always reaffirmed I was doing my best within my circumstances.

A few times we again asked Steve again to join a session, though most of the time he disagreed with Dr. Anderson.

As I worked to renew my psychological strength and sense of identity, my determination to get physically well intensified. Hope slowly returned that finding an answer to my debilitating illness might be possible.

Meanwhile, through Dr. Anderson's encouragement, I regained my driver's license. It had been so long, they could find no record of me ever having a license, so I had to start at the beginning, taking both driving and written tests all over again. That was a huge step for me. I felt like I had conquered a beast when I walked out of the highway department, although I still didn't drive much. Even driving around the block scared me. I was convinced I would have an accident or pass out. At the end of a counseling session one evening, he said he thought it would be good if I practiced driving the next week. Terrified, I agreed.

Knowing Dr. Anderson would be in the car with me made it less stressful. My panic attacks were less intrusive as long as someone accompanied me. This was especially so during driving. I felt like if something happened to me (like passing out), there would be someone to get help.

Steve drove me the next week, as usual, but he waited in the big yard and played with the boys while Dr. Anderson and I took the car.

To my surprise, he asked me to drive to the grocery store where I had my first attack. Now, that did make me nervous, but we talked the whole time. When we got to the store, Dr. Anderson instructed me to walk to the back of the store while he waited at the front. My legs trembled, but I did it! I walked to the back and then to the front again. I felt stronger after that.

As we drove back to his office, he said I was a very good and confident driver. Those words always stuck with me, and I repeated them through the following years when I ventured out to drive.

Dr. Anderson challenged my idea that I would pass out or cause an accident. "So what if you pass out while driving?" he said. "You would have a few seconds to know it's about to happen, at least long enough to pull over to the side and put the car in park, if necessary. You wouldn't stay out long, and then you would wake back up. You won't die ... you'll be okay. There's nothing to it. As a matter of fact, what you're so afraid of rarely even happens."

So, I told myself that over and over again. After I started driving more, even years later, I drove in the right lane when possible so if I needed to turn in somewhere or pull over, I could. But being responsible for our two boys, two precious little lives, in the car with me when I drove overwhelmed me. The chance of something happening to just me differed than knowing something might happen to my precious cargo as well.

Mother and Daddy thought having a cell phone (called car phone at the time) might help calm my driving anxiety. There were probably fewer than two dozen car phones in Anderson at that time. They weren't sold here, but my parents heard about a man who owned a car wash who took orders for them on the side. They purchased one for me and paid the monthly fee.

I was grateful for the phone when I drove, but I was also embarrassed because people could see from the antennae on my car that I had one. Everyone would think I was wasteful. I didn't know of anyone else who had a car phone. As a matter of fact, car phones were just starting to be heard of. My phone had to be ordered from Greenville, South Carolina.

Dr. Anderson understood my panic attacks and helped educate me on them. Maybe you've experienced panic attacks. If so, you probably realize it's not just a purely mental condition, as some people consider them—the effects are very real to you and your body.

A panic attack affects the blood pressure, heart rate, and breathing. God has created a "fight or flight" mechanism within our bodies. These feelings are what you might feel when you are in an emergency situation like a car crash, danger, or even sudden loud noises.

You often hear that a chemical reaction happens in the body when a panic attack occurs. That is true. Adrenaline is released causing a physical, chemical reaction. This can make your arms, hands, legs and feet go so numb you can hardly feel them. Your heart pounds, your blood pressure rises, you just feel horrible. This is what a panic attack really is—adrenaline being released into your body.

When you are weak and depressed, and trying new drugs, these are all things that can come into play causing a panic attack.

You will not die. You will be okay, and you will come out of it. You may need some medicine to manage your symptoms as I did in the beginning … but, please believe me: although it's probably the worse feeling you'll ever have, you'll be fine!

If you fight this instead of accepting that it is coming and working through it, your anxiety can cause the adrenaline flow to be worse. Try to take deep breaths, because often we take very shallow breaths when anxious. Know that anxiety will reach its peak and then taper off, although you may feel like you're in a never-ending state that is getting worse and worse.

Knowledge is your friend; understanding what is happening to your body makes it easier. Your willingness to learn what is going on, as well as the willingness of your friend or spouse, is a huge step in helping you change the entire direction of this panic attack or feeling.

Many times when I started driving again, my fear alone would begin to bring on another attack. I would pray, and I would talk out loud. "Satan, leave me now! You are not in control of my body. My Lord is! I command you to leave in the name of Jesus Christ, whose blood was spilled at the foot of the cross for me! You have already been defeated, so leave! I am out having a good time today, and I flatly refuse to let you ruin it!"

Believe me … this works. My thoughts, my love, and my understanding are with you as you experience something like this. Along those same lines, in his first letter to the Thessalonians, Paul wrote, *Encourage those who are timid. Take tender care of those who are weak. Be patient with everyone* (5:14 NLT).

But the fruit of the Spirit is love, joy, peace, patience, kindness, goodness, faithfulness, gentleness, and self-control.

GALATIANS 5:22-23

Dr. Anderson did so much for me during the year I went for therapy. With his help, I had rediscovered Nancy. My only regret is

I wish he'd talked more about God's presence no matter what I did or tried. I don't remember him talking about God's promises—how He would always be with me and take care of me. I feel and receive that now so I know how important it is.

I wish Dr. Anderson had reinforced this precept in my mind, because at the time, I felt all alone. Even when Steve was around, and I depended on him so much, I still felt alone.

In my head I believed in God's presence. I prayed over and over, but my faith lacked. Oh, how I wish I had felt His presence then as I do now! My life would have been so different.

Chapter Seven

"Come to me, all you who are weary and burdened, and I will
give you rest. Take my yoke upon you and learn from me, for
I am gentle and humble in heart, and you will find rest for
your souls. For my yoke is easy and my burden is light."

MATTHEW 11:28-30

ndy joined Matt at Whitehall Elementary the next fall.
Most days, I couldn't drive them to and from school
even though it was only six minutes from our home. Just
thinking about it defeated me. I had only been able to drive
around the block since regaining my license.

Steve took them to school when he could. Other days, Mother
helped out. I still had to lie down in the morning and afternoon
to regain my strength to deal with two little boys, who were full of
energy when they arrived home from school. I had a friend who
lived nearby and her son was a friend of Andy's. He also attended
Whitehall Elementary.

When Mother couldn't pick up Matt and Andy, I called that
friend or a neighbor. This probably happened once or twice a week.
Oh, how I hated having to ask someone else to do what I should be
doing. After each call, I'd hang up crying.

One afternoon, after calling my friend to bring the boys home, I lay down for a while on the couch after lunch like I did every day. The sun would shine through our big living room window and warm me. I was always cold and shivering. My muscles trembled through my stomach and abdomen until I got warm. That day I got up about the time the boys should be arriving home, but they didn't show up. I thought my friend might have run an errand after picking them up. About thirty minutes later, I called her house, and she answered. I asked if Matt and Andy were there. To my dismay, she had forgotten. She was apologetic and offered to go get them.

What a failure I felt like! My little first and second grade boys were waiting alone in the school parking lot. Everybody else had gone home. Even the teachers had left. Matt and Andy didn't have access to a phone, so they couldn't call.

I just broke down, falling down on my knees and crying. "Why is this happening, God?" I prayed. "Why can't I just get in the car and make myself do what everybody says I should do? I don't understand. Maybe they're right. Maybe I'm not physically sick. Maybe it's all in my head. I'm just a weak person and can't force myself to do this."

I engaged in that kind of self-talk all the time, just really down on myself, which made everything worse. Being a good mother was the one really important thing I had been sure I would do in my life. When my little boys arrived home that day, they were upset, but soon forgot. I never forgot this day—the day I failed as a mother.

My marriage continued to deteriorate. We needed money. My illness took everything we had. We used credit cards and got deep into debt. I prayed every single day that God would help me think of some way to contribute, even with my limitations.

One day I saw an ad in the newspaper for phone customer service for a carpet cleaning company. So I called and, after an interview, I was hired. My job was to phone people and give them a little spiel about the carpet cleaning service, about how we'd come out and clean a room for a low price to get them acquainted with the service. Even though the owner was a nice Christian man, I couldn't continue the job. I felt like I was bothering people. People don't like solicitor calls, and I didn't like doing them. I only took the job because I felt like I had to do something to feel productive and bring in a little money.

During this time, I rediscovered my passion for art. Steve's drafting table in our den had a slanted top where I could paint and draw and immerse myself in art. The first thing I painted was a colorful picture from a magazine of a landscape looking across a field at a circus with tents, people, elephants, balloons, and striped roofs.

I worked on that picture for a long time. It took my mind away from the pain and stress of my life. God had given me a talent for art, design, and color, and when I could escape to that world, I felt better. I didn't earn any money, but I started to feel stronger. My doses of pain medicine were a little more stable which improved my mobility and my stamina.

Then I came across a magazine picture with wooden tulips affixed to stands. Suddenly, I wanted to build that stand. I drew a tulip with the leaves and then cut it out with an old, cheap jigsaw. Uncle Harold made me a belt sander to sit on a table. We didn't have a garage or closed in area, just a carport on the back of the house. I put my tools and wood in the middle of it. We'd have to walk around it when we went out the back door, but I had something to do that made me happy for the first time in years.

After the boys went to school each day, I'd spend the morning working on my crafts. When I came inside, my face and nose covered in sawdust, I felt like I had accomplished something productive. It was always important for me to have something to show for my day.

I mastered cutting out flowers then sanding them with the belt sander and painting them. I made checker boards with cut-out hearts on the outside then stained and painted the squares for the checkers. I bought checkers from a catalog of unfinished wooden supplies and painted one set blue and one set red. This was when the country motif was in style. My friends asked me to make wooden pigs or flowers—anything wooden for their shelves. I'd make shelves with knobs which would hold candles held together by ropes.

One of my friends suggested I do a craft show at the recreation center. So I did. I was excited to finally be showcasing my work and earning money at the same time. I was very anxious, but Steve and the boys went with me. There's no way I could work a craft show all day Saturday by myself. That was the first time I had made money in many years, so it inspired me to make more items to sell.

Steve supported me and always went along to help. He was thrilled I finally had something productive to do that might help me feel better. So he didn't mind giving up a Saturday every now and then to help. My crafts had to be boxed up, and we had to take in our own tables, chairs, and screens to hang items on.

The craft shows were a nice diversion, and the skills I acquired would later lead to successful business ventures. I began taking a supplement recommended by a friend. It consisted of magnesium and malic acid and was called Fibro-Care. With this supplement and the addition of pain patches, my muscle pain became more manageable. I felt better some of the time. Counseling sessions with Dr. Anderson had helped me regain some of my self-esteem. On good days, I drove the boys to school and attended their extracurricular functions. Andy played baseball, and later he and Matt both played basketball.

But the one area that didn't improve was my relationship with my husband. The stress of chronic illness affected our intimacy. I felt like I had damaged something precious. I had killed something in our relationship because I was sick. I could see the little closeness we had left slipping away each day. Many things disappeared right before my eyes.

I should've done better, I'd think. *I should've fought harder, should've seen more doctors.*

I always felt like a failure, though I'd fought hard for my life and my health. I look back now and see how hard I fought through the dozens of doctors and medications I tried. But I couldn't see that then. And though our physical intimacy wasn't what I felt like it should be, I realize now Steve loved me in his own way throughout it all, or he would have left. Why couldn't I see that then?

Steve would come home from work in a good mood and would play with the boys, but he was very indifferent to me. I didn't feel cherished or loved. I wasn't even sure he cared about me. He grew more impatient with my illness. I'm sure by then he felt I should simply be over it. So our relationship had become one of coexistence. Our dialogue had dwindled to, "How was your day?" "I was busy today. How about yours?"

If there were any discussions about my health, it was me saying, "I had a bad day today. I hurt more." By then he had probably grown as tired of hearing that as I was of saying it. Of course, I couldn't blame him.

With most chronic illnesses, marriages suffer. Often, the one who's not sick just can't take it anymore, so they leave. Or sometimes the one who's sick can't take it anymore, and they take their own life. The divorce rate is over 75 percent among the chronically ill.

I prayed, read my Bible more, and cried to God. I wondered why God didn't answer me. I wondered why He didn't help me and He didn't help me find the right doctors. Why couldn't God show Steve how I needed him so desperately? God could change things in an instant, in a twinkling of an eye. I knew he could make my husband understand.

God is doing far more in our affliction than we know at the time.

Even so, life had to go on. I felt blessed with what we did have. Our two beautiful children. Steve's job. The fact that our parents were still alive. I had sisters; Steve had brothers. We live in this beautiful world God has created, but I felt I couldn't join in and be a part of what life should be.

Steve was involved in Cub Scouts and other activities for the boys. We hosted meetings at our house where they built slot cars and did other fun activities. I couldn't help out nearly as much as I wanted, but I was there enjoying the sounds of laughter of our children and their friends.

I worried because the boys were getting older and wanted to go places during the day where they needed someone to drive them. I tried to hide from them the horrible things going on inside my body and head. I made excuses when they wanted to go to a friend's house and I couldn't drive them. Or when they wanted to start playing baseball or another sport that was played during the day, I encouraged them to find one at night when Steve could take them and on good days I could tag along and enjoy our children. Those were the times I could pretend nothing was wrong, and we were a happy, healthy family.

Matt was now eleven years old, and Andy was nine or early in his tenth year. They'd bring home notes from school for special programs they'd want mothers to volunteer to help with. For holidays like Thanksgiving, the teachers asked the mothers to make special foods. I made up excuses when I couldn't go or participate. I never said I was sick. I didn't want Matt and Andy to think I was different from their schoolmates' moms.

Since he was one of the youngest in his class, Matt should have started in the first grade a year later, so we moved him to a private Christian school with smaller classes, allowing him to get more individual attention. This meant I had to drive further each day. I tried not to rely on Mother, but some days she'd still have to pick him up.

I started attending church again. The boys were old enough to go into their classes, sit with their friends, or sit with me. At first, I arrived right before the worship service and sat near the back in the sanctuary, in case I had to get up and leave. Dr. Anderson gave me a strategy to get through. He felt I put too much pressure on myself to succeed at things immediately, which set me up to fail. He told me not to plan to stay the whole service, just through the music and, before the preaching started, leave.

So I returned to church the way Dr. Anderson suggested. I didn't expect myself to stay the whole time. I sat on the back row where I could slip out after the music, if need be, without calling attention to myself. Even if I had to leave early, when I'd get in my car to drive home, I felt stronger, like I'd really accomplished something. And I had.

Those first few times, as I sat looking up at the choir and the pastor, I could see Steve in the choir where he sang. My vision was double and blurred at times, so I saw two of everything. I kept blinking my eyes and thought what a horrible feeling, but I wanted to be in church. I wanted to listen to the words of the songs, stand and sing those words, and have them touch my heart. I wanted to hear the pastor, and I wanted the words that he spoke to encourage me and give me strength and determination.

It was difficult to get all that out of a service when before I'd get there I'd have diarrhea and be so weak. Just getting to church and sitting on the back row was a chore. All that was on my mind was, *I have to do this. Lord, help me do this. I just wanted to be able to be there and worship.*

Steve became more involved in church since I was driving more, and the boys were a little older. Church leaders asked him to be in charge of activities, and of course, he did because if they asked, it must be God's will. He was a deacon often. They'd rotate on and off, but any time he was eligible, he was a deacon.

He was involved in the men's group. He loved singing with the choir, practicing for special events and performing duets and solos. All this required him to be there before and after choir practice, at least an hour or longer.

I was so proud of him. He had such a special God-given talent to share with others, but the more I tried to attend, the more uncomfortable I became. Mother and Daddy attended, along with many other people who knew about my illness and had opinions about it. I always felt like people watched me, whether they were or not.

I longed to be involved in a church where people didn't know my past and where women weren't drawn to Steve. Though I initially feared attending a large church, I began to embrace the idea that leaving our small neighborhood church for a larger one might be the fresh start we needed.

While we wrestled with this decision, I muddled through with a mixture of good and bad days. I took several prescription medications each day for nerves, IBS, and pain. These prescriptions and the Fibro-Care were beginning to help. They kept me functional, but my quality of life was barely tolerable on some days. I'd been sick for almost a decade without a diagnosis. My sessions with Dr. Anderson had come to an end, so I was without a therapist for the time being.

A close friend and pastor talked to Steve and me about going to another church when we confided our problems in him. Steve agreed to start visiting other churches. If this could help me to get better, he was willing to try.

Somehow I convinced myself that starting over in another church—with a clean slate—was the answer. That way, I would be able to muster the energy to pull myself together and start living the life I felt my family deserved. I only had to try harder.

Chapter Eight

You and your loved one's suffering may be inscrutable today.
But in reality it is preparing for you or them "an eternal weight
of glory beyond all comparison" (2 Corinthians 4:17). Take heart
and hold on. If God feels cruel today, you will discover someday that
it was a pain-induced mirage and that He had graces planned
for your joy beyond anything you ever dreamed possible.

JON BLOOM, *When God Feels Cruel*

After visiting several churches in Anderson, we started attending Concord Baptist Church in 1984. Matt and Andy got involved in RAs and the youth group, but they weren't comfortable there. Their friends went to other churches. Most of the kids at Concord attended T. L. Hanna High School or McCants Middle School. The youth pastor, Randy Blank, did everything he could to make them feel welcome.

Steve and I attended prayer meeting together on Wednesdays while the boys participated in their activities. And then for a while, I was able to attend our Sunday school class with Steve. It was nice being able to go together. But, after sitting for an hour in Sunday school, it remained hard for me to attend the worship service right after. Sometimes I did. Other times, we took two cars, which allowed me to leave before the worship services.

Even though I kept struggling each week to attend church, I was determined to be there. I wanted Steve to know I supported him. I would see him looking for me when the choir would come out. He was always looking. I never wanted to miss hearing him sing. But sometimes I had to leave before he sang because it made me so nervous. I remember standing in the vestibule, looking through the glass in the door to watch and listen to his beautiful voice. Other times, I'd be bolder and walk in and lean against the back wall of the sanctuary and listen. My heart would be pounding and my legs trembling, but his words and voice would fill my heart with joy. But I always felt a sense of never being worthy enough to be married to such a wonderful man. He deserved so much more than a sick wife who could not support him in all the things he loved to do.

I prayed, "Lord, please let me be here for the right reasons. Please let me hear my husband's beautiful voice with which you've gifted him. Please let him see me standing here smiling and supporting him. Let him know how much I love him, and that I want to be here."

A battle waged within me all the time. Sometimes I told Steve that. Other times I didn't. I was so sure he was sick of hearing about my problems when he'd walk into another room in the middle of a conversation.

I was still having virus-like attacks where I'd become extremely weak with muscle spasms. My muscles never completely relaxed. Anytime I strayed from the norm, whether it was sitting in a new chair, walking upstairs, or riding in a different car, my muscle spasms increased. Once, when we changed cars, my right leg and hip pain worsened for many months. My menstrual cycles worsened to where I'd be almost debilitated the week before.

Steve and I joined Weight Watchers, and I started losing weight. I tried to walk for exercise and realized I couldn't walk on any type of an incline nor could I walk very far. I didn't venture too far from the house because it increased my anxiety. I was hospitalized during the late 1980s with kidney stones and diagnosed with hypoglycemia. I continued to be treated for anxiety with Vistaril and Tenormin.

Steve and I began to discuss building a house. It had always been our dream. Steve had been blessed with several pay raises. I earned a little money from crafts. Not much, just enough to have spending money and then put the rest into buying more wood, supplies, and paints to make more crafts.

The more we talked about building, the more excited we became. We'd lived in the house on Woodside about ten years. Even after we decided to go forward with our plans, we questioned whether we could afford it.

We looked at house plans, but I didn't see any I liked. After we bought a wooded lot in the Brittany Park subdivision, I decided to draw our house plans myself. I used Steve's drafting table in the den and drew the plans on drafting paper. I picked different ideas from rooms I liked in housing magazines and put them together to design our house. It gave me something exciting to do, something I enjoyed and looked forward to each day. I spent over a year doing this. I measured each room as I worked on paper, which showed me the correct dimensions of each room.

I started to walk more and began to feel a little stronger. Actually, after we bought our lot, for several months the fibromyalgia subsided enough that I could work and do some things. The pain patches helped tremendously. I also think, without realizing it, when I controlled my diet like I did on Weight Watchers, it greatly affected my undiagnosed celiac disease, which in turn lessened the effects of fibromyalgia. I had not equated the two diseases at that point, because I had no idea fibromyalgia existed, nor did I realize how food factored into my muscle spasms and bouts of viral symptoms and debilitation.

Steve became more interested in the house plans as they developed. He was proud that we'd bought land and decided we'd save money if we cleared it ourselves. The boys and I went to the lot many nights with Steve after work to help clear it. The boys and I had loppers to cut small bushes and trees. Steve had a chainsaw to cut the larger trees. I could lean over to cut bushes and drag them to the street, which was a tremendous accomplishment for me. I'd be sore the next day, but most of the time, I managed without severe side effects from the strenuous activity. This was an exciting time in our lives as we began our new home. The whole family was involved. In June of 1988, I started working part-time as a secretary at a local church—my first real job working outside our home since before Matt had been born. Through this job, I became acquainted with a lady named Shirley who worked for a dear friend and his wife. They were very involved in the church and asked that she help me with some of the tasks that were new to me. I learned quickly, and I enjoyed being able to get out, and to also bring in a little extra income. The boys were now in high school and old enough to stay at home if I had to work after they got out of school, but my hours grew far beyond what I expected.

I became overwhelmed with many duties I wasn't prepared to do, and soon I was given the job of putting together their Sunday bulletins. These took hours per week to construct. The church didn't have a computer. I had a typewriter and a copier, so I would type information in sections, copy it, and then use glue sticks to stick it onto a sheet of paper. The church bought bulletins with a front printed on them, not like the ones today. I would write up the articles and type them out, then for the headers, I'd put each section on the copier to enlarge it. They had a clip art book, so I made copies of hymnals or music notes or youth activities and glue those onto the bulletin. Once I got all the pieces compiled and on the bulletin page neatly, I'd make copies and then fold each one by hand.

I felt overwhelmed as my work hours grew, but I couldn't bring myself to think about quitting.

One day, Shirley mentioned she'd seen my art at a craft show. She was impressed with my wreaths and wooden crafts. She'd seen my artistic flare from the church bulletins I created. She asked if I ever thought of owning my own business. Of course, I hadn't. I had been barely functional for almost a decade. Besides, I had no money to invest. But my own business? What a dream come true it would be! Although I didn't think it was possible, I was interested in hearing what she had to say.

When I told Shirley I didn't believe I was financially or physically able to run a business, she brushed that aside. It seemed I'd been getting stronger. She offered to put up the initial financial investment and buy the merchandise and give me a small salary. That was a big investment to put up in the beginning, knowing we would not make any money for quite a while. My contribution to the business would be to run it every day, except Monday, and her contribution would be her investment.

I considered her proposal. Could I do it? Would we attract enough customers by selling my crafts and wreaths along with what Shirley purchased at market to be successful? Was I feeling well enough to be responsible for keeping a business open five days a week? I thought just maybe I could handle this.

Shirley found an empty store across from the former recreation center in a tiny strip mall downtown. So, in October of 1988, I agreed to go into business with her. Although nervous about doing so, I was excited for the opportunity to fulfill my dream of expanding my career in art.

I learned a lot about running a business, but it didn't succeed like we'd envisioned. I also learned another valuable lesson, namely that partnerships can be tenuous at best, so about six months later, we agreed to part ways.

A well-known florist, The Straw Basket, was on the market, I heard. Located near the mall, The Straw Basket had a good reputation in Anderson. Their stock of merchandise was somewhat diminished, but there was cottage-style rustic furniture for enticing, eclectic displays, beautiful wreaths, and rolls of ribbon that I could work with. On June 1, 1989, we made the decision to purchase The Straw Basket. Steve and I secured a loan from the bank for $30,000.

I couldn't run the shop by myself. The former owner, Debbie, agreed to stay on for a while as an employee to help get things going. And the young woman whose family had previously begun The Straw Basket agreed to work a couple of nights per week part-time.

It was getting close enough to the Christmas season to go to market in Atlanta and order merchandise for fall and Christmas. Since the shop's name hadn't been changed, Debbie went to Atlanta with me and used the store's reputation to make purchases from the large vendors so we could get Christmas dating. This means you buy merchandise in the summer and don't pay for it until December 10. Steve and I were excited to be going somewhere by ourselves. I'd not been well enough to do anything like that for years.

I depended on Debbie's advice and experience as she suggested what needed to be ordered, what would sell, and how much we'd need for the Christmas season. On that first trip to market, I probably spent $60,000 to $70,000. After we returned home, the merchandise started coming in, more than would fit into our small storage room.

Debbie suggested we open a kiosk in the Anderson mall. With the help of my other employees, we could make more wreaths and assorted Christmas products to sell. I'd move merchandise and make my money back even quicker with an extra outlet. And, at that time, it seemed as though I felt well enough to tackle a second location. Debbie and I went together to talk to the mall manager. He said he had an even better idea. He had a vacant store. He'd let me have it for the same price as the kiosk, about $1,000 a month for the Christmas season. So I signed a short-term lease, and we moved in.

I then realized more employees were needed at both stores and that I should order more merchandise. I ordered $150,000 in total that Christmas. The mall store was open seven days a week. I tried to work in both stores as much as possible. I still had spells where

I felt like fireworks exploding in the back of my head, and I'd have to sit or lie down or I would have fainted.

Debbie then thought it would be a good idea for me to do the holiday fair, an exclusive Christmas craft show for our area, in Greenville that year. It was a three- or four-day event from nine in the morning to ten or eleven at night. Someone had to man that space, too, plus set it up with tables and screens to hang wreaths on and display merchandise.

Debbie's husband, Dave, helped in the mall store. He was so helpful and never asked to be paid. Steve even came to ring up people at the mall store at night when I didn't have enough people to work there. Besides Susan and Debbie, I hired five others to work part-time. We sold a great deal of merchandise. I thought, *Wow, this is great, we're making money,* but I was surprised that we still ended up with a shortfall after Christmas.

I realize now that I had taken a chance with each of these decisions. Not only did I think I could purchase and run my own business, but I thought I could handle an extra location in the Anderson Mall with many long Christmas hours. Then, to top it all off, I actually thought I could also handle selling at the largest, most prestigious craft show located in the state. I felt more like a normal person than I had in a long while. I wanted to make up for lost time, and besides, I loved what I was doing.

With Christmas over, it was time to order spring merchandise. I had no other choice because I had no way to pay the bills if I didn't keep selling. I had begun digging a huge hole. I didn't know at the time how much debt it would put us in. Debbie and her husband went to market again with us. We stayed for three days, with Steve and me paying all expenses, which had to be put on credit cards.

Spring merchandise arrived, and we worked hard to make beautiful wreaths and arrangements, but the store wasn't profitable.

I fell behind on the rent payment. The landlord came by to talk about how I was going to pay the rent. I'd pay him what I had, and he'd come back another day for more. My dream had turned into a nightmare. I couldn't see any way out of the situation.

Even as the stress mounted, those around me, including Steve, encouraged me to continue. The idea of an upscale gift and floral design store was a good one. The Straw Basket had a good reputation, so I'm sure everyone thought I was clearing a huge profit. But the truth was I was so far in debt I didn't envision ever getting out, and I got further behind each month. I also felt guilty that I wasn't at home with Matt and Andy. I had thought I would have more time with them, but they were teens and ready to do things on their own.

I became obsessed with this business debt and worked hard to get out from underneath it. We had a new house and bills to pay. Reality finally set in, and I worked up the courage to talk to my landlord, telling him I couldn't pay the rent. He'd been firm up to that point but was very kind and generous in letting me out of the lease. We agreed on a settlement amount, which was much less than I owed him.

I totaled all the merchandise in the shop, but it wasn't enough to pay the agreed amount. About the time despair set in, a solution walked through the door. Another opportunity in another strip mall. The owners came in asking me to move my well-known shop across town to their newly remodeled strip mall. The first two months' rent in the shop would be free, and I'd have reduced rent for a year after that. The shop would be bigger, and it'd be a way to recoup all I'd lost and still keep my business.

Exhausted and with no other solution in sight, I agreed to their offer.

Chapter Nine

Because of the Lord's great love we are not consumed, for his compassions never fail. They are new every morning; great is your faithfulness.... The Lord is good to those whose hope is in him, to the one who seeks him; it is good to wait quietly for the salvation of the Lord.

LAMENTATIONS 3:22,23,25

My hopes were still high that I'd get out of debt and make a success of The Straw Basket. I had become more business savvy through this ordeal, although so much of my debt rested on the economy at that time. I also had to face the fact that the business did not have enough inventory on hand to cover the purchase price I paid—I put a lot of stock in the name and reputation of the business. I'd become a master at wreath making through experience and coming up with my own creative ideas. But nothing had changed in my personal life except I wasn't home as much. Steve seemed to be okay with that—he wasn't home as much either.

Before we switched churches to get a fresh start, our pastor friend from Pope Drive Baptist told Steve to reprioritize his life. If he wanted to keep his marriage and family intact, it was necessary that he put God first, family second, and church third. No matter what our problems, neither Steve nor I ever wanted to jeopardize our family. He gave up choir and many other activities so we could attend another church together as a family.

Because we were involved in Weight Watchers, we ate better. The lack of constant activity between church and home, and Steve joining me for church each Sunday, reduced a great deal of family stress. Working in my shop enabled me to be productive and feel like I contributed in some way. Although I hadn't been diagnosed yet, we now know all of these things make such a difference in the lives of people with celiac and fibromyalgia. The less nervous and stressed I was, the less depressed I felt. The more balanced my life, the more balanced my health.

I had survived those initial years of acute illness. When I worked in The Straw Basket and the boys were teenagers, I felt better. In fact, these were probably the best years I had experienced as an adult.

I was able to stand on my feet more as I worked. I couldn't take anything for pain except Advil and Tylenol. I had begun taking twelve Advil per day along with the twelve Fibro-Care I'd taken for so long. I went to the chiropractor often, sometimes four or five times a week. His office was within a block of The Straw Basket, so I'd go during the day or after work. He's a major part of the reason I was able to work those long holiday hours.

Still, I couldn't keep my weight down, even on Weight Watchers. I tried walking for exercise, but I'd have to walk somewhere flat without an incline because if I didn't, the muscles up the back of my legs, into my back, shoulders, and neck would spasm and hurt. I never understood why I had to increase so slowly when walking. Doctors would say, "Just start out at ten minutes. That should be easy." I finally didn't even explain to them anymore that walking only two minutes was an ordeal for me.

I don't know how many years I experienced improved health. I worked really hard every Christmas season with extra hours, sometimes five or six nights a week, even after I'd moved the shop into the Durham Shopping Center, closer to downtown.

I managed to make it through Christmas every year, but my body would totally crash afterward. Then started the days I had to leave work early or couldn't work at all. I ate unhealthy food the weeks of Thanksgiving and Christmas, but I also pushed myself so hard in the months preceding that the punishment I put my body through always caught up with me.

The dizzy spells with the explosion-like feelings in the back of my head continued. If I couldn't sit or grab hold of something, I would've fallen. Those happened often. I'd suffered inner ear problems since my teens, but this wasn't the entire reason for these terrifying spells. If I moved suddenly, bent over for too long, stood on a boat dock, or climbed too many steps, I got dizzy. If I stretched to reach for something that overstressed my muscles, I'd get dizzy.

Despite these issues, the years in the early 1990s, between my acute onset of illness and before I hit bottom again, were relatively good. I maintained a functional level of discomfort, but I was productive. I'd learned not to stress my muscles by bending or reaching too much. If I did, I often had to rest at home for a few days until my muscles weren't as tight. I kept a stool behind the work counter, where I could sit to make wreaths when my legs couldn't endure anymore.

Most of the years since the boys' births, we did little in the way of family trips or vacations. I couldn't ride in the car any great distance nor handle the stress of how poorly I felt most of the time.

Once, friends offered us a house on Hartwell Lake, which was only a twenty-minute drive from our home. We loaded up the car like we were going on a vacation—the first in many years. Steve took the boys out on the lake to fish in our friends' small boat. I sat in a folding chair by the lake to watch them fish, or I sat on the screened-in porch and looked down at them. With no place to eat out, I cooked three meals a day. The house sat on a hill with a footpath that wound down toward the water, so you didn't have to walk straight down or up. I remember slowly walking this path with Steve's help, when only a few years before I couldn't walk more than a few feet up or down steps.

The inconsistency in my health conflicted in so many ways with our lives. I understand how Steve stayed confused. Sometimes I could do nothing, and other times I did activities that surprised even me. This contrast in my abilities fueled Steve's belief that nothing was truly wrong with me. How could I blame him? I wanted him to understand, but even I didn't.

Our second vacation was at Hickory Knob State Park, a little further away in Abbeville County. Steve's family reserved rooms for us to spend the weekend together. The park had a pool, a golf course, a game room with pool tables, and a dining room.

Everyone enjoyed the pool, especially the children. On two occasions I ventured down into the water to swim, something I used to love. I had been a great swimmer in fact. But this time, as I stood in the water, moving very little, the muscles in my legs grew weaker and weaker and started to contract.

As I slowly climbed the steps from the pool, it was all I could do to get to the top step before having to sit. I sat until I could hold up the weight of my own body. I didn't understand. Why was this happening to me?

To sit on the sidelines knowing something was terribly wrong and wanting to be normal was so difficult. But, I did as I always did. I wore a disguise that had so often become me—a fake smile, laughter, and chit-chat while I was falling apart inside. I wanted to enjoy myself like everyone else. I didn't want to talk about my health or lack thereof. I only wanted to be normal and have fun.

I have often heard many say that fibromyalgia has been called the disease of "the great deceiver." Most of us do learn to talk, laugh, and smile, and can join in with a group when necessary when inside we are severely broken and falling apart. Now that I think about it, no wonder people don't believe you're really sick.

A continual battle raged within me between my desire to be a good wife and my desire to work. I wanted to earn money. I had such a strong desire to be more involved in church and a good Christian—the kind of child of God that other people around me appeared to be. But my body constantly got in the way. Sometimes I had the strength to fight harder, and I'd be able to do more. During those times, I stayed as active as I could—I would suddenly have a burst of strength and desire to make up for lost time—but I always overdid it. Other times, I'd be overwhelmed by pain and stress, which caused me to get weaker with depression as a result.

Even with the best doctors I have now, I can't specifically say what caused me to cycle back and forth like this. What helped me to go to church one Sunday and not the next Sunday or the next? What allowed me to have a spring or fall where I could enjoy the outdoors and walk? The most I ever managed to walk was a third or half mile, and it took a lot of walking to build up to that, but I was proud of the accomplishment. The cycling back and forth between good and bad days is one of the mysteries of fibromyalgia. Now, with my amazing doctors, and their explanations, this is not so much of a mystery anymore.

When I could barely go anywhere or do anything, Steve would drive me to the door of a store and let me out, so I could save my energy and steps for inside. If what I wanted to buy was in the middle or back of the store, there would be this internal struggle. I would start preparing myself before I arrived.

Stress played an important part in this, as well as anxiety, but that was more self-induced because my mind anticipated how my body typically responded to situations, and the anxiety of anticipation made me weaker. All this self-talk went on in my head continually.

If I go in Belk's and walk way over to the makeup counter at the other end of the store, what if I can't walk back when I'm finished?

So while I'd be trying to walk through the store, my anxiety would increase and make my legs weaker. It was a vicious, vicious circle—one I still fight, but to a lesser degree, to this day.

I'd been waging a battle of struggling and sinking, sinking, and sinking, and struggling to come up for air. But I truly think God gave me strength when I didn't even know where it came from. He comforted me when my illness became too much for me to bear. He put his arms around me and held me, putting salve on my wounds, as I experienced warmth and comfort when my husband didn't have it to give anymore. You see, the pain we had both suffered had killed much of what we felt years before as that young couple so much in love.

The pain was never completely gone. If I did too much, naturally I hurt, and there was always a limit as to how high I could reach with my right arm. Sometimes the object would be so close, I thought maybe just a little more and maybe it won't hurt my back. But every time I overstretched, I had muscle spasms all the way down my back. It started in my neck, then spread to my right shoulder, wrapped around to my shoulder blade, down my back, into my knees, and into the tops of my feet. They'd become totally numb.

If I did anything I knew I shouldn't do, it could set me back for a couple of months. I knew how many times I could bend over and pick up vases of flowers on the floor or lean over and pick up something or reach for something. I pushed myself, thinking maybe if I did it two or three more times, I'd be through with the task. So bending over at the shop had the same effect; it would take me months to completely get back to my "normal" baseline of discomfort and function.

Sounds strange, I know. When I tried to share this with Steve, he found it hard to believe. He would say, "You were doing all of these things yesterday or the day before. Now you can't move, go anywhere, sit anywhere, or bend over."

Steve is a good man with a good heart, but this shows how a debilitating, chronic disease can affect and change every member of a family.

His bewilderment hurt me, but I had no explanation for my fluctuating health.

I didn't realize it at the time, but part of the problem was that I was malnourished because of the celiac disease. The word conjures up an image of frail, thin, emaciated people, but you can be overweight and malnourished because you're not receiving nutrients, vitamins, and minerals to your muscles. When I tried different supplements, at first my body didn't process them correctly so I could absorb the proper nutrients for my benefit. On the day of my sixty-fifth birthday, after recent bloodwork, my doctor told me I am finally not malnourished anymore.

I don't think eating one bad meal would've made a difference, but during Christmas or Thanksgiving, I'd eat more than one bad meal in a day, and then we'd eat leftovers for days. My body would crash every January, partly due to this bad food. Back then I cooked macaroni pie, sweet potato casserole, chocolate cake, cobblers, and pies. I cooked a lot of unhealthy food, but that's what Steve and I grew up eating.

Whatever the reasons, I enjoyed the two or three times I had the burst of energy to sustain me long enough to get something major accomplished. Once, with the help of a salesman, when Steve was out of town, I spent an entire weekend moving heavy metal shelving and merchandise to restructure my store and stockroom. I didn't know where the energy came from, and I was sore on Monday morning as anyone else would have been, but not like I typically would be if I pushed myself too hard.

I was grateful for the spell of wellness that gave me beautiful memories of clearing our lot in Brittany Park with Steve and the boys. I was grateful to see my dream come to fruition of having a career in art. These memories sustained me during the difficult times. It gave me hope that maybe there was an answer to my health issues. I only had to keep trying to find that answer to the riddle; after all, something gave me energy and strength at the most unexpected times. Were they signs from God that I shouldn't give up—that He had so much more in store for me?

In 1997, Steve and I took a vacation to Nashville, Tennessee, to watch Matt's band play at the Dove Awards for Christian Music. After that, we were blessed to be able to go on a free vacation to Cancun, Mexico, with Steve's cousin and her husband for a long weekend. That was the first time I had ever been on a plane. Also that year, we traveled seven or eight times to Atlanta and Charlotte to visit their gift markets.

Eventually, as it always did, the overactivity caught up with me, and I began to have more bad days than good. I was rushed to the emergency room with chest pain and diagnosed with gallbladder disease, resulting in having to have my gallbladder removed. It didn't help, but this surgery (although minor) was one that seemed to take me forever to recover from.

After this surgery, the Vistaril I'd taken for so many years suddenly wasn't effective anymore. My doctor doubled the dose, and it did nothing. So, he switched me from Vistaril, adding three new medications all at once: Desryl, Klonopin, and Prevacid. I never felt as good again taking these new medicines as I did on the older one. The next few years continued in this cycle of spurts of wellness intermixed with extreme pain and sometimes debilitation.

My work situation rapidly deteriorated as well. I'd been at Durham Shopping Center for a few years and getting deeper in debt and more behind in the rent. At the end of each year, Steve and I had the same discussion. I needed to close the store. I owed more than I could sell it for. I owed more than the merchandise which filled the shelves was worth.

Steve would always say, "Let's keep trying." He knew I loved doing it, and I did. But I should have stopped many years sooner, before we got to the point where desperation took over. Now, it was either close the doors or find yet another place to move into.

The store accounts were delinquent. We talked with a bankruptcy attorney to help us sort out the finances of The Straw Basket. He said he saw no way out except to file bankruptcy, but we refused and ended up digging our way out by selling our house. Every penny was used to begin paying off the huge mountain of debt. Our dream home that we had planned and built together years earlier was sold. After paying off as much debt as we could, we found a nice house to rent.

I still had a business and some inventory, and most of all, I still wanted and needed to work. I began looking for a new location for my business with less overhead. If the business was to survive, drastic changes had to be taken. I tried taking some of my wreaths and crafts to local consignment shops. I took a few to a consignment shop out of town where I had rented a space with my sister.

During this time, I met two nice ladies who, as partners, ran a large women's cooperative together in downtown Anderson. One sold antiques and garden furniture, and the other sold new home décor items from the Atlanta market as well as antiques. The business consisted of over 250 consignees selling a large mixture of inventory. They offered to make a place for me in their business, to share their nine-thousand-square-foot space, so I paid a fairly large sum to become a partner. My overhead would be reduced dramatically and I quickly saw it as my only chance to keep The Straw Basket going while I struggled to continue paying off debt.

We received so many compliments as the shop now became "Straw Basket at Brook Green Court." My arrangements, wreaths, and crafts looked so inviting in the cute vignettes we put together and designed.

As a couple of years passed and my business partners grew older, they wanted to be free to travel more with their husbands. So I became the managing partner, handling the money and taking care of all the paperwork, consignments, and customers. My hopes of sharing expenses didn't materialize as anticipated. I still had to pay my employees because I couldn't manage everything. We were busy, with many customers, but the profits just weren't there. I muddled along because I didn't know what else to do.

As I struggled to keep the shop afloat, my marriage was still in trouble. Steve and I traveled on parallel emotional paths. Though he outwardly supported my business ventures, we weren't connecting on any level. If I needed something done or something moved at the shop, he'd come and do it. He worked really hard many nights, helping me rearrange large pieces of furniture and more small accessories than you could imagine.

No matter what, no matter how deep the financial hole the business was in, he always wanted me to keep the shop. He'd never seen me feeling physically better as when I had the shop. He'd never seen me that happy or busy or being productive, but it also kept me busy enough that I worked a night or two each week in the off season, and many more during Christmastime. I should have realized this gave Steve a lot of free time, which isn't good for any marriage. Yet he seemed genuinely happy for my emotional and physical improvement.

The boys graduated from high school, and though I didn't know it at the time, I was headed into the most difficult period of my life. A period marked by death, betrayal, and my biggest struggle yet to survive.

Chapter Ten

*"Come to me, all you who are weary and burdened,
and I will give you rest. Take my yoke upon you and learn
from me, for I am gentle and humble in heart, and you will find
rest for your souls. For my yoke is easy and my burden is light."*

MATTHEW 11:28-30

Even though I couldn't figure out how to fix my marriage or make my shop profitable, I had gained a renewed self-worth through owning The Straw Basket and making wreaths. My work was important. Or so I told myself. It gave me a reason to push myself beyond what I imagined I was capable, but the shop took time I could have spent with my husband and family.

It was easy to get caught up in customers' compliments and the sense of accomplishment I felt as I offered more than my customers expected. After all, God gave me the talent, so all the nights I worked late, I felt justified in doing so. Steve said it was okay; it didn't matter. When guilt crept in, I'd call, and he'd encourage me to keep working late.

"It's fine, just don't wear yourself out. Don't work too much." A few nights were as late as ten o'clock, and Steve would call saying, "Are you ready to come home?"

If I were by myself, Steve would drive to the shop, especially when the store was located downtown, where people loitered on the street all hours of the night. When he arrived, he'd blow the horn for me to lock up. By then my energy was spent. I was tired and Steve was tired. I should have focused more on him, but I don't know if that would have made a difference at that point.

Steve seemed perfectly happy with our life. I didn't sense he wanted more from me. In fact, I sensed that when I was around too much, I was in the way. We were like two strangers living in the same house, which is what chronic illness creates.

When I felt really bad, the chronic illness made me focus on myself. It made me concentrate on the pain day and night. The pain was my reality, my broken heart was my reality, and feeling rejected from God was my reality. Sure, I prayed, read my Bible even more, and jotted down inspiring verses, but I couldn't see a response.

So I continued in my own little world at the shop. I received affirmation from that job I didn't receive at home from my family, from church, from God, or from Steve. I'm ashamed to admit that because that's not what my life on earth is for or about.

When I first got sick, I prayed every single day, "Lord, please, please, please show me what I've done wrong. Show me the person you want me to be, what you want me to do. Tell me if I'm not being who you want me to be, and I will become that person, Lord. Just tell me, and I will."

When I look back on those years now, focusing on some of the times I felt better, God was giving me a chance. But instead of turning toward Him, getting involved in church, being a better mother or wife—I put all my energy into the business. Maybe God gave me those chances, and I blew it. I know life's not that simple. Chronic illness never is. God was with me, however, and as a spiritually immature Christian suffering great pain, I couldn't see through the fog to understand that. So I kept doing what I knew to do and moved ahead.

Steve, on the other hand, had gotten heavily involved in church again. He sang in the choir, the praise team, a couple of quartets, and his band. He also had many extra work projects requiring late hours.

During this time, my parents' health deteriorated rapidly. Several years earlier, my dad had retired after working at Duke Power for thirty years. He enjoyed his retirement and felt well for a while. He worked on projects like building a carport and was so proud of it. Not long after that, he got sick. He went from one doctor to another, but they couldn't pinpoint the cause of his problems. His feet and legs were numb all the time. All the years of working in appliance sales and moving washing machines and dryers had caused back injuries. The after effects of those injuries had accumulated, causing the nerves inside his spine in the lower back to be compressed. The doctors thought they could go in and chisel off part of the spine that pressed on nerves going down his legs, and his pain would stop. So my parents traveled to Atlanta for Daddy to have surgery at Emory.

Mother was very weak herself. She always weighed less than a hundred pounds, probably nine-five pounds then, but when someone got sick, this inner strength came up from within her. She did what had to be done. No matter how she felt, she selflessly took care of my father. This corresponded with the time I was in the beginning of my most acute illness phase.

After years of Daddy's health deteriorating, Mother started going downhill too. She started losing more weight. I can't bear to look at pictures of them at that time because they were both nothing but skin and bones. Even though my health had improved enough that I had returned to work and bought The Straw Basket, helping to look after them while trying to run a business and take care of my family sapped what little energy I had.

They often needed groceries, which I couldn't even buy for my family most of the time. Even so, Mother resisted us taking over anything she perceived as her job as the homemaker. But it got to the point where she just couldn't go. So Steve and I tried to do the shopping for both families at once. We'd go to her house and make a list of what they'd need for a week. Mother became agitated if we bought more canned goods or meat that would need to be frozen instead of kept fresh. We couldn't get her to understand it was easier on us and really made no difference in the way she ran her kitchen or kept house.

I'd go by and check on them in the mornings on my way to work and again on the way home. One day, I dropped by unannounced at lunch. Mother was a stickler for three cooked meals a day. It broke my heart when I walked into their kitchen and saw Mother and Daddy sitting at the table, eating corn and green beans out of cans. Even with canned vegetables, she had always cooked them for three hours like she did fresh, with a little corn oil, salt, and pepper. She always cooked meat, had Jell-O, and then dessert.

That day she didn't expect anybody to stop by. I'll never forget walking in seeing them eating those cold green beans and corn out of cans. By that time, my daddy just did whatever he was told to do. After years of sickness and pain, dementia had now set in. Mother was really upset because she knew that wasn't the way she'd always done things. When I asked her about the food, she got highly insulted.

I didn't want to leave, but I had a business to run, so I called my sister who lived in Anderson to go over. Mother had done so much for me and for us when I was sick. I left there knowing I had to go back to work. I had employees relying on me and orders to fill. Steve and I faced mounting debt and had to keep the business afloat, yet Mother and Daddy were eating out of cans. What else was going on when I wasn't there?

That evening, I talked to Steve about their situation. Though we had our problems, Steve was sensitive and thoughtful when it came to my parents. He always asked how he could help and did anything he could.

My sisters were both married with children and jobs, and one lived over an hour away in Greenwood, South Carolina. I was the oldest, so I felt it was my responsibility to take care of the situation. We hired a sitter for Daddy to relieve some of Mother's stress. She railed against this. No one could take care of him like she did. Then she began to accuse us of taking her things or putting them where she couldn't find them. The biggest problem was her driving. We tried to convince her it wasn't safe, but she wouldn't listen. I'd get calls during the day from businesses where we knew the employees, and they'd say, "Your mom is here and doesn't know how to get home."

So I'd leave work and go pick her up or sometimes call Susan. Steve and I managed to convince Mother to let us have power of attorney and help her make medical and legal decisions. We took her to the doctor. They diagnosed her with Alzheimer's, though a definitive test for that diagnosis only comes after death when the brain can be analyzed. Little was available in the way of care or answers for Alzheimer's patients or their families twenty years ago.

One day, I told Steve and Susan, "We have to talk to Daddy. He has to be aware of what's going on."

So we sat down and told Daddy, "You know Mother's not well."

Very matter-of-factly, he said, "Yeah, I know. She has Alzheimer's."

We'd never mentioned it to him before. He didn't show much emotion except to say, "Yeah, I know." He'd probably known all along but wondered what their lives would be like or how her diagnosis would change their lives.

We hired sitters to stay with them both twenty-four hours a day.

One would stay until the next arrived for their shift. They cooked meals and cared for Mother and Daddy.

If something happened during the night or a sitter called, Steve or I had to be ready to run over in a moment's notice. We didn't have young children at home like my sister who lived in town. If a problem came up during the day, the sitters would call me or Susan at home. It took going through more than thirty sitters before I found three amazing Christian ladies. Some of the ones I let go worked a day, some a week or two weeks or several weeks or several months, but something always happened that caused me to let them go, or they quit. Once we caught a lady stealing as she left. We'd drop in at odd times to find a sitter in the backyard smoking and not watching my parents. We'd drop in at mealtimes, only to find their meals were not what my parents should be eating. I couldn't let that go on. I just couldn't, but when we let someone go, Susan, Steve, and I had to care for them while I frantically looked for another sitter.

I'd hired as many people as I could to run the shop while I went back and forth, trying to be the best daughter, mother, and wife I could, fighting anxiety and pain daily, and doing whatever I could for my parents. But for all my efforts, I would still leave their home crying every day. We would get calls in the middle of night, sometimes from Mother and other times from Daddy, with questions about the sitters like: "What's this woman doing here? She's not supposed to be here."

In April, Daddy fell and broke his hip. After making sure he was okay after his surgery, we left one of his sitters to stay at the hospital with him. We got a call in the middle of the night that his condition had worsened. Susan and I went to the hospital. Daddy's breathing was very shallow. Sitting by his side, we thought Daddy would make it and be fine. He didn't and died that night.

We didn't tell Mother that night. She was in her bed asleep with a sitter in the other room. Susan and I went over to her house the next morning. She was dressed, had her pocketbook and coat ready to go see Jack. I couldn't tell her that we couldn't go. Susan had to tell her. She didn't seem to understand at first. She just stared at us for probably five minutes, and then broke down and fell against Susan and cried and cried.

Mother had been fighting Alzheimer's with all her strength so she could take care of Daddy. Even with the sitters there, she watched everything they did. She still wrapped his legs in hot towels and plastic and rubbed his legs every day, no matter who was there. Without him to care for, she deteriorated rapidly.

Not long after this, Steve surprised me when he came home from choir practice saying he had signed us up to go on a cruise with about twenty others from our church. That would be for our twenty-fifth wedding anniversary. We were to join our friends for a nine-day cruise to the Western Caribbean. We'd paid a big down payment. Honestly, I didn't think I'd make it, but at the same time I saw how excited Steve was and how he wanted to go on this cruise. I thought, *So what's going to happen? If I fall apart, they'll just have to knock me out. If I can't walk somewhere, I'll just have to stay in the room. If I die, it's just my time.*

So three months after Daddy died, we went on the cruise. Susan checked on Mother, and we still had the same three sitters. Sandra also drove up from Greenwood to help while we were gone.

The cruise was wonderful. I was able to do things I didn't think I could do. Steve wanted to do activities like others were doing like scuba diving or hiking to the Mayan ruins or walking up and down the hills of the streets of the Grand Caymans. I couldn't do those things, but I could walk some, though it had to be on a fairly level surface without many hills. I did enough that I thought we had a really good time. Steve laughed a lot. He probably paid more attention to me that week than he had in a long time.

When we got home two weeks later, Steve still talked about our twenty-fifth anniversary vacation. Even though I was thrilled with the closeness Steve and I had experienced for the first time in a long time, nothing changed at home. It wasn't until years later I discovered the impact of our trip wasn't the same for Steve as it had been for me.

My mother's health continued to deteriorate. The Alzheimer's had taken a toll on her body, and she suffered a heart attack. Against our wishes, we were forced to place her in a nursing facility but still paid the sitters to stay with her around the clock. We couldn't bear to leave her there all alone.

After several episodes of the nursing home staff not caring for my mother properly, one of the sitters begged us to let them care for mother back at her own home. She had been with Mother there before and knew it was the right place for her to be. She said, "We can take much better care of her there than any other place."

That was a really difficult decision and such a huge responsibility with the condition Mother was in, but we did it. By then she stayed in the fetal position, having not talked or even moved her legs, hands, or arms for several weeks. So we decided to move her into the den that had been Daddy's bedroom. We got a hospital bed and turned it to face the big picture window that looked out over the big backyard with pecan trees and azaleas and pretty green grass. She had gone for several weeks without any response or any eye movement in the nursing home, but when they rolled her into the den, put her in the bed, and turned her so she could see the yard, she smiled.

Hospice came in daily to care for her. I stopped by her home each morning to sit and talk with her, but she never acknowledged me. Susan came by after I went to work, and sometimes Sandra would drive from Greenwood while her children were in school. I came by again to check on her on my lunch hour. Then I stopped on my way home from work each night to talk to her and make sure she had everything she needed.

Honestly, I had nothing left for my husband. His feelings for me had turned off many, many years before when I got sick. I too had learned to turn off my feelings so I didn't get hurt anymore. We were like two strangers living in the same house.

Mother passed away in October after struggling so long to stay alive. Hospice workers felt like she hung on so long because she felt we needed her. Susan, Sandra, and I gathered around and told her good-bye. We also told her it was okay to join Daddy. Within hours, she slipped away.

So 1997 was a horrible year, a year I don't really want to remember. It's the year that Matt and Andy both moved out of the house at the same time to go to college. It's the year that I'd hoped would be good in my marriage because, for the first time in a long time, Steve and I had enjoyed vacations together, both the cruise and a beach trip. I thought the cruise would bring us closer together, but it didn't.

Although Steve says he loved me the whole time, our entire marriage, that no matter what, he always loved me, that was the year he decided he needed to enjoy life. Another decade passed before I became aware of his decision and discovered to what extent I had been betrayed.

Chapter Eleven

Jesus looked at them and said, "With man this is impossible, but with God all things are possible."

MATTHEW 19:26

I was still grieving the loss of my parents and the fact that Andy and Matt both moved out of our home at the same time to go to college. An empty nester for the first time, my world was falling apart around me. I struggled to stay afloat, both physically and at the shop. My spells of pain lasted longer, and my peaks of good days were much lower than they used to be. I struggled to handle normal everyday activities.

In 2001, doctors found another cyst on my remaining ovary. This time I needed a hysterectomy. I was terrified, because I remembered how the last surgery to remove my gallbladder had such a profound effect on my health. And now this.

My recovery was long and drawn out, as was the case with the gallbladder surgery, I never seemed to fully recover from the hysterectomy either. I did discover that, while on antibiotics immediately after the operation, my muscles responded differently; they didn't spasm as much. So the surgeon put me on a Z-Pak two times a day for three months. Even though I was still having a hard time recovering from surgery, my muscles began feeling better and not cramping as much during those three months. I hadn't felt this alive in years. Then the doctor wanted me to stop taking the medication for a while. My health deteriorated quickly. My doctor agreed to let me start back several months later, but this time, I didn't experience the same relief.

Desperate, and in excruciating pain most of the time, I even tried a massage therapist, which made the pain worse. She said she could barely massage my back, and when she did, my muscles felt like they were on fire. That's what happens with a deep tissue massage, she explained. "I can just barely touch your back, and I feel the heat. I don't want to hurt you, so I don't think I can help you."

In 2002, I began seeing a different doctor in Anderson, who suggested I may have fibromyalgia due to food and environmental allergies. She did skin tests for environmental allergens but not food. I tested positive for trees, grass, weeds, dust mites, cockroaches, and mold. This doctor was surprised at the strong reactions I had to the scratch tests on my back. One of them made me ill, and she had to give me a shot to counteract it. I had no idea what fibromyalgia meant at that time, and she didn't explain. Dr. Lane said I may have some sort of genetic disorder she wanted to test me for, but when I went for a follow-up visit, she never mentioned it again. Nor did she offer me any solutions, except the medications Zyrtec and Nasocort. I just added her observations to the list of all the other unhelpful suspected diagnoses I'd received over the years.

In addition to my other medications, I continued to take twelve Advil a day while we were right in the middle of building our second home. We had worked hard, saved, and a large bonus Steve received from work made this possible. I made an appointment to see a pain specialist whose wife had been a frequent customer of The Straw Basket. She had observed my struggles, though I'd tried hard to mask my pain in front of customers. For some reason one day, she and I started talking, and she said her husband was a pain specialist. She was sure he could help me, and she called, getting me an appointment right then without a referral.

I tried not to get my hopes up too high. I'd seen so many doctors who I thought could help. At the first appointment, the doctor reassured me that he could help. My heart soared. I wanted to believe him. I wanted to be out of pain.

He tried a TENS unit, which is a device strapped around your waist and back that sends little electrical shocks to your back muscles. It was a very expensive treatment that didn't work for me, and insurance didn't cover it. He switched to Lidoderm pain patches, starting with one a day on my back. The patch relieved the pain in the area around it, but the pain radiated to other muscles, so the doctor increased the usage to two a day. Then my right hip pain grew worse, so he increased it to three patches a day. Steve would help me put the patches on in the morning before he went to work at six o'clock, and then he'd remove them around ten o'clock at night.

The pain relief was temporary and sporadic. Sometimes I would have to go in the bathroom and sit and cry and then attempt to fix my makeup, come out with a smile, and try not to let anybody know. I heard about a neurologist in Seneca, about a thirty-minute drive from our home in Anderson. I don't remember where I heard about Dr. Rossi, but he'd been recommended as being experienced with fibromyalgia, so we made an appointment to go see him.

Dr. Rossi was very kind and encouraging. He never attempted to diagnose my ailment specifically as fibromyalgia, but he assured me he could treat my pain. I went through the same ups and downs of getting excited, actually believing a doctor, yet knowing deep inside it wasn't true. It was difficult not to hope when I was in so much pain, yet I just couldn't let myself believe this was the doctor who might finally make a difference in my life.

Dr. Rossi told me to continue using the Lidoderm pain patches. He gave me a different medication to try, maybe more than one. Each medicine didn't work, or it was so strong it knocked me out, one or the other, until one day my pain got so bad, I didn't think I'd survive.

For years, Steve would rub his hands up and down my back very gently. I couldn't take much pressure at all. But I had found that if he gently rubbed my back, I'd get a little relief. He knew how hard to press. Sometimes he did this in the morning before work, when he got home from work, or before we went to bed. The gentle rubs gave me temporary relief and took the edge off my pain, but overall, my condition worsened. I couldn't identify anything different in my routine for my health to be declining so rapidly.

One day, when Steve came home for lunch, he rubbed my back and felt the knots in my muscles under my right rib. I remember this day so well. We were sitting on a small couch in our tiny den. I asked him to rub a little harder, thinking it would release the muscle tightness. The chiropractor was closed that day, so I couldn't get a treatment from him. It felt good while Steve massaged it, but when I stood, a muscle spasm grabbed me with such force that I couldn't breathe or move. I could only whisper. The spasm wrapped all around my body and underneath my rib. I couldn't take a full breath.

Steve stood at the door, ready to leave for work. I asked him to wait so I could get to the bed and lie down for a minute to get relief. I leaned down to touch the bed to sit, and the pain at that moment became more unbearable than anything I'd experienced in my entire life.

I screamed for Steve to help me. I couldn't lie down, and I couldn't get back up. He came in and pulled me up. I was screaming. I managed to sit on the side of the bed while Steve waited.

Finally, he said, "I really have to get back to work."

"No, something has to be done now. I have to go to the ER or something."

"Tell me what you want to do."

I thought about Dr. Rossi, so I called his office. He was getting ready to close for the day, but he said if I could get there, he'd wait. I took two or three Xanax and several Tylenol or Advil and also put ice on my ribcage. Steve put a couple more ice packs in his lunch bag to take with us. I didn't know if I could make it to Seneca, which was forty-five minutes away, but I'd been to the ER so many times in the past, and I knew they wouldn't know what to do to help me.

We left for Seneca. I remember having to sit very still and not turn my head. I tried not to breathe too deeply. When we arrived at Dr. Rossi's office, he examined my back and asked if I could stand completely up. Of course, I couldn't. I walked leaning over and limping because of the pain, which went all the way down my leg.

Dr. Rossi and Steve helped me sit on the side of the exam table. Dr. Rossi gave me a nerve block injection in one muscle and then told me get up and walk around. The main muscle had loosened a little, but others all around it were still in spasm. Then he gave me another injection a little further down in the same muscle. The pain started to subside. Before he was finished, Dr. Rossi had given me six shots. He said they would wear off in two to three days because it was for symptom relief. The shots did nothing to actually address whatever caused the extreme pain. He was right. In a few days, I returned for more shots. I'd seen the chiropractor in between, but it didn't help.

This time Dr. Rossi said, "We can't just keep doing this. We've got to do something that will last longer."

He wanted to try Botox, which is used primarily for cosmetic purposes. I'd never heard of Botox used for pain. He said he'd have to order it, and it would be very expensive. A small bottle that cost about $1,200 would yield about twelve injections. We scheduled an appointment to return to his office in two days. When we arrived, Dr. Rossi said the bottle of Botox was at a pharmacy in Walhalla, a neighboring town, so we drove to the pharmacy.

Once there, we learned our insurance wouldn't pay for the Botox. Steve and I stood there trying to decide what to do. The pharmacist said we could file the expense through insurance later to see if it would be reimbursed, but they couldn't let us have the Botox until it was paid for. Steve and I decided we would have to put it on our credit card.

We drove back to Dr. Rossi's office with the Botox bottle, and he started giving me injections of it. It was like he was chasing the pain. He'd give me a shot in one place, and the muscle quit hurting. But then the pain moved.

"How was that?" he asked.

"Well, it still hurts here." I pointed to another site.

"Let's give you a shot there."

A lot of this was probably as much me as it was him. The injections made the pain stop, so I continued to point out places where I hurt, and he continued to inject. Finally, he stopped and told me to take the bottle home and put it in the fridge because I had several doses left.

When I stood from the exam table, I felt really weak. He assured me the effect would wear off. When we arrived home, I could hardly turn my body to get out of the car. Steve had to hold onto me and almost lift me up the three steps to get me into the house.

That started three to four months of hell. I called Dr. Rossi and told him I hadn't recovered and how extremely weak I'd become. He said sometimes Botox will do that. Sometimes the effects will stay in your muscles and make you weak. He told me I would just have to wait until it wore off. Once later he called me and admitted he probably gave me too much Botox.

I could barely walk from my bed to the bathroom. Every now and then, I'd make it to the den and sit in a comfortable chair, but it wasn't often. The ladies at the shop had to work more to keep it open. Steve had to go by and pick up the money to make deposits and bring it home to me. I'd sit with it in my lap and try to write out the deposit because Steve had never handled the finances, either at home or with the shop. I had juggled bills back and forth between business and personal accounts for years, trying to keep us afloat.

After a couple of months, I went to work when I felt a little stronger. Just to drive to the shop and sit was a huge accomplishment, but I stayed as long as I could, maybe three hours, before I had to leave.

While I was struggling to come back to work and stay as often as I could, a couple of employees told me how another employee was complaining about having to work extra hours while I had been out. She was another who thought I was being lazy, that I should make myself snap out of it and come back to work full-time.

That was it! I'd had enough, and it broke my heart because I had always thought so much of her. My two other partners were out of town again, so I had really pushed myself to go in as often as I could, and stayed longer than I should. I wasn't able to work, and I shouldn't have been there. But I'd been sitting on the stool and then standing a little while adding a few stems to a wreath. Every now and then, I attempted to walk the twenty feet to the cash register to ring up a customer. Then one day, the same employee made a snide remark directly to me, which broke my heart even more.

I went home feeling down and depressed. Steve wasn't home. He was at church a lot those days and out of town on business many others. He was gone quite a bit during that time.

The next morning, I woke up and thought, I can't do this anymore. I can't believe the people I care about and trust don't believe I'm sick. The employee was one more person added to the list. I won't do this. I just won't.

So I drove to the shop, walked through the front door, and told the employees I was closing the business. Their reaction was what I expected—anger, shock, hurt—but I couldn't turn back once I finally faced the reality that Straw Basket at Brook Green Court had to close.

I didn't waste any time; within a couple of weeks, the going out of business sale started. Consignees had to be notified to pick up their items or they would be sold at a reduced rate. My partners, who had been out of town, were upset when they returned, but at the same time, they were not willing to take on the responsibility I held for too long.

We dragged it out as long as we could to bring in as much income as possible in the last few months. But, the day finally came when around nine thousand square feet had been emptied. The full downstairs and the main floor, which had held so much merchandise, were cleared out. The final task was to box up materials and other remaining supplies and to move it all to my home studio.

That last day, as I stood on the sidewalk beside the once inviting, eclectic storefront business, I put the key in the door and turned it for the last time. That chapter of my life was over. I was saddened. I felt lost. *I will not give up,* I thought to myself as I walked to my car. *God has given me a gift—one that I'm good at and have confidence in. I will continue somehow, some way. I'll see what tomorrow will bring.*

Overwhelmed by lingering grief from my parents' deaths, my boys moving out, and the final blow of losing my shop, too, I began to feel life slipping away. Depression gripped me along with the downward spiral of my health.

I clung to any thread of hope someone offered me. One such thread came from an acquaintance who'd been through a divorce due to chronic illness. She recommended a therapist she thought might help me.

Steve went with me a couple of times to see the new therapist, but the therapist said Steve was not the one who needed help—it was me. *Here we go again. All the problems are always mine. What am I doing wrong?* So, I continued to see him by myself, still trying to find a doctor who believed I was truly sick and could offer a real diagnosis.

We had begun building our new home, one I had designed, so we moved into a small duplex apartment while we built. Things between me and Steve were worse as I could feel tension rising. Steve had never shown his emotions, but I began to see that he was upset, worried, and tense. Probably for the first time ever, Steve raised his voice at me more than once. I was in shock, I was upset. What was going to happen to us?

Lord, please save us. Please save our marriage. Is it too late? Lord, if you heal my body, maybe I can fill this void in Steve's life ... and in mine. I had to keep my thoughts and my mind on the new home we were building, or I wouldn't have made it. I had to focus in other directions to keep my sanity. It would be years later before I understood what was happening in his life at this particular time.

The one bright spot in 2003 came when we moved into our new home. This time, at Steve's suggestion, we also built a workshop across the breezeway from the house so I could work from home. I hired my previous assistant, Kim. Even though I couldn't physically make wreaths, we collaborated on their design and she created them. I rented space in an upscale consignment shop to continue selling wreaths. I kept praying I would be able to stand or sit at an easel to design wreaths again one day.

I told Kim I had an idea. I was going to sell wreaths on the Internet.

"Are you serious?" Kim said. "You don't know how to do that!"

I had no clue what it involved, and I couldn't find anyone to teach me or talk to me about my new venture, so for the next two or three months, I read everything I could get my hands on about Internet businesses. At that time, eBay was my only option. So I searched through all the help features on their website, set up an account, and started reading about how to list and sell an item.

Considering I knew nothing to start with, there was more to it than I'd imagined. Just creating a very simple listing took me a very long time. Then I had to figure out how to ship my designs. How would I get my large wreaths into a box? Once I found the right size boxes, how would the wreath be secured for shipping? I spent months trying to figure out the process. Fortunately, I could do that sitting down. I had an older computer, but it was good enough to research and start reading.

By the time I got eBay figured out and began listing my wreaths, I had purchased a more up-to-date home computer with faster Internet access. I also spent a lot of time surfing the Net in search of a diagnosis and solution to my health problems. I refused to let the doctors' and my family's apathy and begrudging acceptance of my poor health defeat me.

Sandra and Susan both had some health problems as well, but not like mine. Their encouragement was all I had sometimes. They were the only ones who truly believed I was physically sick.

My sisters spent many hours researching on their computers as I did on mine. We searched for others that had the same symptoms I experienced, looking for answers to my problems. As I researched, I experimented with many supplements in addition to the Fibro-Care. Some helped, and some did not.

One day, I came across the word *fibromyalgia*. There was that word again I had heard before so I began to read more about it. Doctors had suggested so many diagnoses to me over the years—everything from housewife syndrome to Lyme's disease—but I'd only ever heard the word fibromyalgia in passing from a couple of doctors. They'd made it sound so unimportant, as if it were like the common cold. My chiropractor had once mentioned myalgia, but a real diagnosis had never been pursued by any of the medical professionals treating me. I continued to research until I found a doctor within driving distance who specialized in fibromyalgia treatment.

On December 12, 2003, with my research in hand, I arrived at St. Francis Hospital in Greenville, South Carolina, to see a woman doctor who specialized in fibromyalgia. I had taken a chance and called to see if I could make an appointment without a referral. God was looking out for me that day, because they made an appointment for me quickly. At that first visit, the doctor read through my file, making note of my food and drug allergies, my reactions to things in my environment, my unusual fatigue, and my joint and back pain. She then did a thorough examination. As result, she confirmed that I was suffering from a severe case of fibromyalgia brought on by allergies.

Did I dare get my hopes up that this could be the elusive diagnosis I'd spent decades searching for? If it was, how would knowing help? I knew from my research that neither doctors nor society seemed to give fibromyalgia sufferers much respect. In fact, many believed the symptoms were psychologically driven, much as "housewife syndrome" had been suggested to me decades before by more than one doctor.

Despite all the years of defeat and dashed hopes, I did dare to hope; I couldn't help but hope. Somehow, with the help of the right doctors, I would find the path to wellness and restore my life, my marriage, and my dreams. I'm glad now I didn't know the devastating direction my life would take before my hopes became a reality.

Chapter Twelve

I waited patiently for the Lord, and He inclined to me and heard my cry. He brought me up out of the pit of destruction, out of the miry clay, and He set my feet upon a rock making my footsteps firm. He put a new song in my mouth, a song of praise to our God. Many will see and fear and will trust in the Lord.

PSALM 40:1-3 NASB

Around the same time I went to St. Francis Hospital, I learned about a family doctor who was a member of our church. The first time I saw him, he listened to all I'd been through, and then he told me something I'd never heard—words I'd waited decades for someone to say to me.

"I do believe you're sick, and I'm sorry you've had to go through all of this. But, I'll tell you up front I don't know a lot about fibromyalgia. If you want me to become your doctor, I will. If, through your research, you discover a test you want done, or some drug you want to try, then we'll discuss it. You probably know more about what's wrong with you than I do."

I knew I'd found the doctor for me—the one who believed me and trusted in me. He is still my doctor today and has said many times: "I'm not exactly sure what you're finding on the Internet, and I don't always understand what your doctors in Atlanta want you to do, but … you're getting better, so just keep on doing whatever it is that you're doing."

So my doctor and I have sort of an understanding. Even when he doesn't think we should run a specific test or I should take a certain medication that had previously helped, we talk through the situation, and he agrees to try.

In September 23, 2004, based on Susan's and my Internet research, I asked my doctor to test me for porphyria, an enzyme disorder. I tested positive. Porphyria symptoms are very similar to those experienced in fibromyalgia. No doctors in Anderson specialized in treating porphyria, so my doctor referred me to an oncologist. He couldn't explain why I tested positive, and at first, he thought all my problems could be coming from porphyria. He wanted me to see a specialist at the Kirklin Clinic in Alabama.

I don't know how I got there or back. We had to spend the night on the way there, and also on the way back. I was weak and in severe pain. We had to pull over several times so I could get out of the car and walk around or even just stand and stretch. I took a lot of pain medicine in order to make that trip.

After all his testing, we learned I have acquired porphyria, which is different from regular porphyria. And, it probably was caused from everything else going on in my body. It was a side effect of fibromyalgia and not the direct cause of it.

For about three years, I saw my family doctor in Anderson every three to six months. I still took Fibro-Care (twelve per day) and other supplements my research led me to think might work.

Meanwhile, since I had started feeling somewhat better—and after several months of researching eBay and how to ship wreaths—I believed I could actually have an online business. So, I began listing wreaths on eBay late in 2004.

Then in 2006, I learned about a fibromyalgia specialist through

Stephanie, our son Andy's wife. When they first met and were dating, she told me her mom also had fibromyalgia. She had been seeing a doctor in Atlanta who had helped her. Her regimen including giving herself shots in the stomach every morning, consisting of 60 mg of magnesium, 10 mg of folic acid, 30 mg of B-12, and 20 mg of B complex.

I talked to Stephanie's mom, got the phone number of her doctor, then called to find out if he did phone consultations because I couldn't make the two hour trip to Atlanta. They agreed to a phone consultation on February 16, 2006. Dr. Beckham was so kind during that initial conversation. He is an elderly gentleman, and as I got to know him, I discovered he's a Christian. He often talks about trusting and turning our situations over to God.

We'd talked for about forty-five minutes when he said: "You have celiac, which has caused your fibromyalgia. If you go on a gluten-free, soy-free, and lactose-free diet, I believe you will improve."

Surprised, I asked if he planned to do any sort of test to prove his diagnosis. He said oftentimes the test gave a false positive or negative, and if I tried the diet for two weeks, that would be all the proof we needed. Not knowing the extensive list of foods that negatively impacted my body, getting my celiac under complete control and thus, having a positive effect on my fibromyalgia, would take longer.

I don't know why I didn't start the diet right then. I suppose I had a hard time believing it would make such a difference. I'd had so many false diagnoses that something as simple as changing my diet to relieve my symptoms seemed unbelievable. It seemed there should be something more to help.

Eventually, I tried the shots, which I administered in my stomach every day for a few months. I didn't notice a discernible improvement, though. We later discovered I'm allergic to that form of B-12.

After about three months, I called Dr. Beckham and agreed to try the diet, which wasn't as simple as I'd thought. When I didn't know what to eat, I just didn't eat. Finally, I thought I had it figured out yet didn't feel much better. He asked me to keep a record of everything I ate for one week and send it to him. He returned it with red "No's" and X's all over it. I still wasn't eating the right foods.

I communicated with Dr. Beckham on the phone for the next three years as I tried to tweak my diet to bring my celiac under control. If I could successfully do this, he believed my fibromyalgia would improve, but it would take time. The obvious foods marked as gluten-free or dairy-free weren't the problem. Whenever Steve and I ate out or bought food, we didn't know if my meal had been prepared alongside foods with wheat in them and thus were gluten contaminated. I had stomach problems after eating out, which resulted in my feeling drained with no energy. If I ordered a burger in a restaurant and they put it on a bun, it caused me problems, so I had to send it back for them to make a new burger.

Most restaurants accommodated me, but the ones that didn't we didn't return to. Many food products such as vitamins and spices aren't labeled as containing gluten even when they do. I went through much trial and error in trying to figure out what I could eat and where. Things are so different now. We can go out to eat just about anywhere and enjoy a nice gluten-free meal. I am still hyper vigilant; if the waitress doesn't understand when I say I'm allergic to gluten, we politely get up and walk out.

Meanwhile, Steve and I started to see marriage counselors in Greenville. As my physical health improved, I had begun to realize the depths of our unhealthy relationship. Steve had never embraced the idea of counseling, though he always supported my going. But he did agree to see this husband-and-wife team recommended by our church. More often than not, we saw them together. At other times, we saw them separately.

In January 2009, Steve had knee surgery to repair torn cartilage. Once he got him home, still groggy, with his knee wrapped in ice, he insisted on checking his e-mail in our office. After that, he settled down on the couch as I went into the office to print an e-book I'd purchased online. Once my 129-page e-book printed, I brought it to the kitchen counter to punch holes in it and put it into a binder.

As I picked up the final stack of pages, one last page remained on the counter. It could have easily been picked up with the last stack and secured into the binder without me ever seeing it. As I picked it up, I saw …

It was an e-mail Steve had accidentally printed instead of sending. An e-mail meant for another woman. Suspicions I never wanted to let myself believe were confirmed while steadying myself and reading that e-mail.

The next few days brought one revelation after another—the years of infidelity and the lies to cover his actions. He'd been living a double life. It was a nightmare I couldn't wake up from. I couldn't eat and slept very little. I insisted Steve tell me everything, and each uncovered layer of deceit brought more tears and agonizing heartache.

We finally told our children. They could already sense something was wrong, and of course, they were devastated. They asked if they could pray with us as we sat together in our den that night. Those prayers touched my heart forever.

We spent almost three hours with our therapists that following Monday morning delving into the situation. After this long counseling session, it still took Steve days and weeks longer to realize the depth of what he'd done. He'd confessed, promised he wouldn't do it again, and felt it should be over. Case closed. We shouldn't have to keep rehashing it with counselors.

His attitude on our way home that day made me want to jump out of the car right there in the middle of I-85. I reached one of the peaks of my anger at that point, but somehow managed to get home without acting on my emotions. With each measure of forgiveness came another wave of anger, another wave of disbelief that my husband had not only cheated but had done so repeatedly. Yet during our counseling sessions, I came to realize that this is not uncommon in marriages with a chronic illness.

Please don't hear me say there's ever an excuse for infidelity. Forgiving was excruciatingly painful. Walking away would've been easier, in some ways. I would never judge those who do. The pain was greater than anything I'd ever experienced, which is probably why God cautioned specifically about this sin within a marriage. Yet, walking away from a covenant made before God and with God, even when broken by one party, is not something to be taken lightly. Saving our marriage would be difficult, but it was a decision we consciously and prayerfully made. Steve had to be committed to fidelity for us to save our marriage, but in order to heal, we had to address why it happened.

We spent many hours in counseling and discovered the reasons for Steve's infidelity were multifaceted. Among these was that his needs were not being met. Yes, physically at times, but not emotionally either. My own emotional needs had not been met for a very long time. We were strangers sharing a home and a life, but the irony was we both so desperately craved the same thing—emotional intimacy—which was absent.

During the next year and a half, I couldn't work. My design assistant came and made wreaths while I stayed in my office with the door closed and locked. After she left, I struggled to list a few wreaths for sale on Etsy. This was the only work I did for the next eighteen months.

Steve and I plowed through these difficult months with our Christian counselors and also our associate pastor. For the first time in our marriage, Steve and I began praying together morning and night every day. Months went by without the television being turned on. We sold the two recliners in the den and bought a loveseat and an oversized chair called a Snuggler. I can't even begin to add up the hours we sat in the Snuggler or in the loveseat praying, talking, and crying together. We read the Bible, and during this time of healing, we read through more encouraging self-help books than I can begin to count. Each time our counselor or pastor recommended a book, we read it. We learned the meaning of joy in a marriage, and still, to this day, both carry pocket stones imprinted with the word Joy, given to us by our dear friend and pastor, Randy Blank.

The healing didn't come quickly, nor was it easy. Each time I thought I'd embraced forgiveness, there would be another thought, a place, or a moment that would trigger the despair we had faced. Once, we were reading one of the books our therapist recommended and a question came up. At times like that, anger and rage surged through my body like I'd never felt, not even when I first found out.

How could you have done that? How could you have said that? How could you have felt that way?

All I remember is with one swing of my arm I swept all my cherished pieces of china onto the floor. Dents still remain in our floor where I broke beautiful pieces of china, but I didn't care. When you're betrayed on such an intimate level, pieces of fine china don't matter. I didn't care how the house looked. I didn't care that Christmas decorations from the previous Christmas were still up in May. I didn't care if I broke my grandmother's china, which was also on that shelf.

We cycled between emotions where everything seemed to be okay and we'd be happy, then another trigger of pain and devastation would surge or build up inside me again. All I can say is God saved us. God knew we couldn't do it alone as He reached into our lives.

He pruned us and cut us down to where we both knew if we didn't turn to him, we wouldn't survive the pain of this horrible ordeal.

You know the verse from 1 Corinthians 10:13? It says: *No temptation has overtaken you except what is common to mankind. And God is faithful; he will not let you be tempted beyond what you can bear. But when you are tempted, he will also provide a way out so that you can endure it.*

Throughout the Bible, God allowed more trials, more pressure, than His children could bear. The reason God allows us to experience times when we are thrown into a deep, dark pit and consumed by trials that are bigger than we can handle, is so we have nowhere else to turn except toward Him.

Steve and I chose that path; the hard path, certainly not the easiest one—the easiest one would have been to walk away. Steve chose the hard path by staying, loving me, and holding me as tears flowed. I also chose the hard path by not insisting he leave as I let him hold and comfort me while tears flowed. We dealt with more than most couples can live through, but please understand this: it was not by our own power, but through God's grace. We couldn't have done this alone. If you're facing these types of trials, you can't either. Jesus says, "Apart from me you can do nothing" (John 15:15). You are too weak on your own. But through His power, you are strong.

> But He said to me, "My grace is sufficient for you, for My power is made perfect in weakness." … For the sake of Christ, then, I am content with weakness, insults, hardships, persecutions, and calamities. For when I am weak, then I am strong.
>
> 2 CORINTHIANS 12:9-10 ESV

God sent so many people into our lives at just the right time—from pastors to our therapists. We'd already been seeing them for a year and a half before this happened.

I once told our therapist that if we had not already been seeing her, we wouldn't have made it. God's hand had been working in our lives all along. She's helped me understand and open up about my feelings. She helped Steve and me when we reached a wall or a roadblock that stopped us. She helped us break down each barrier by asking pointed questions and being determined to get the right answers. If she sensed we weren't being totally and completely honest, she confronted us openly about it. God sent her into our lives to do that.

Steve and I started a miracle book, which is basically a legal pad filled with notes, times, places, bulletins from churches, names of people who've helped us. Upon picking it up, Bible verses on cards, torn pieces of papers, and tickets from concerts, events, and places we have now been able to attend begin to slide out from all sides. These were things I was able to do that I'd not been able to do before. Each item represents a miracle by God in our lives. All the people that we've encountered who had exactly what we needed at exactly the right moment, those are the ones who've gone into our miracle book. At the top of these miracles is how God changed our lives in the last eight years, both spiritually and physically.

I know God opened my eyes to Steve's feelings and needs that I had closed my eyes to many years ago because I felt unimportant. I felt like I wasn't the right wife for him. I felt like Steve wished he'd married someone else—someone who could be the wife he wanted and deserved. All of a sudden, God brought memory after memory to my mind. I started remembering things Steve had done trying to show me how much he cared throughout our marriage.

There was once when Steve came home and said, "Pack a suitcase. We're going somewhere overnight."

He meant well, but he didn't understand my illness enough to realize an overnight trip terrified me because there were only two chairs in our house that didn't hurt me terribly to sit in.

Instead, Steve would say, "Let's go. You'll feel the same whether you're here or not. You just need to get out of this house."

So he made reservations, and we went to Greenville, which is only thirty minutes from our home. He had dinner brought to our hotel room. The bed was so hard I couldn't lie down because it hurt my back, and the couch was no better. We ended up coming home that night. I was devastated and disappointed. I remember that night like it was yesterday. I cried because I was so sad that Steve had tried to do something special for me, and he felt like such a failure.

In the midst of everything going on in our lives—losing our home, already involved in an affair—Steve still threw me a surprise fiftieth birthday party that he planned from start to finish all by himself. He did the decorations. He planned the food. He sent out invitations. Probably fifty people were in our home that night. You don't do that for someone you don't love. Steve says he loved me all along. I had a really hard time believing that in the turmoil and aftermath of the affairs, but now I do.

I'm sad now when I see what Steve had to give up because of his infidelity. He quit singing in the choir and praise team at church. In fact, we switched churches because the pain, the faces, and the rumors were too much. We needed a clean break from Steve's past. The band he has been with for over twenty-five years is the only thing he kept doing. Everything else extracurricular stopped. There were no more golf trips and even no more Clemson football games until we could go together. He lost so much, but in his loss, he was proving to me how much I really did mean to him. Steve chose what was most important in his life: God and me.

Chronic illness destroys a relationship slowly. You lose something every day. It seems you were close to each other yesterday, but today that intimacy is gone, and then something else is gone the next day.

Most couples get a divorce when it's revealed there's been one affair or maybe infidelity happened once. Our therapist told us that over 90 percent of couples who have been through what we have don't make it.

I can't tell you why I didn't leave except I believed God didn't want me to leave. God didn't want me to make Steve leave. God numbed my mind and my body to feelings, which could have ended it all for us. He saw things going on in our lives that had to change, and no matter how painful, he had to do it. He had grand plans for our lives together—for our future. He wanted us to help and encourage other couples who might be experiencing the same horrific situation that we did. He had to show us what it was like to live the marriage of our dreams because we didn't know what to expect, since we'd never truly experienced it. It's taken many years, but that's what we live now.

We do have the marriage of our dreams. The trust is back as well as a closeness we'd never experienced before. If not for that, we couldn't be sharing our story with you today.

Steve is concerned about me and everything I do and every thought I have. I often overhear Steve talking to others about me: my strength, my courage, and my accomplishments. He talks about how I help women with chronic diseases through businesses that make a difference in the lives of so many God has led me to touch. He talks about what I have overcome, but I talk about both of us being overcomers. What a wonderful feeling that is.

Through it all, the grace and strength God gave us was like an emerging sunrise with its amber and pink rays streaking the sky. You know there's hope and happiness on the horizon, even after going through something as horrific as we'd experienced in our marriage. You just have to hold on until the sun breaks through.

The most amazing day was when Steve came to me and said, "I have to understand your illness. I have to know what it has done to you all these years. You've found a doctor that helps, and I haven't seen or talked to him at all."

Ironically, I had never seen him, either, since he was in Atlanta. I hadn't been able to ride any distance in the car for a long time. Even on some of our trips to Greenville to see our therapists, I hurt so badly that we would pull off at an exit so I could walk around to alleviate my pain.

But God started changing my body along with the changes He'd made in Steve and in our marriage. The first of April, Steve said, "We're making an appointment. Don't worry—I'll get you to Atlanta no matter how many times you need to stop."

For the first time in my life, after decades of despair, I had genuine hope for my marriage and my health—a hope rooted in God's Word and promises. Despite the hard work that lay ahead, the sun had finally begun to shine in our life.

Then your light will break forth like the dawn, and your healing will quickly appear, then your righteousness will go before you, and the glory of the Lord will be your rear guard.

ISAIAH 58:8

Chapter Thirteen

I waited patiently for the Lord; he turned to me and heard
my cry. He lifted me out of the slimy pit, out of the mud and
mire; he set my feet on a rock and gave me a firm place to stand.
He put a new song in my mouth, a hymn of praise to our God.

PSALM 40:1-3

In April of 2009, I finally met Dr. Beckham, that caring, cheerful man with a long white beard, face-to-face. I also met his associate, Dr. Romano, a world-renowned nutritionist who would work miracles in my life in the coming years. I can say with much certainty that I wouldn't be alive today, much less thriving and running successful businesses, if it weren't for these two doctors. Steve stepped forward and arranged my first appointment, saying he would get me to Atlanta, no matter what. It was such a comfort to know that for the first time, together we were eagerly searching for answers to my health issues.

Steve sat in Dr. Beckham's office and explained to him about the infidelity and that it had happened, at least in part, because he didn't understand my illness. Dr. Beckham was very kind and understanding. He had encountered this same scenario time and time again in his practice treating many patients just like me. He's an older man with such a heart for God as well as his patients. He explained to Steve that fibromyalgia is a despicable disease. He said it causes more marriages to break up than any illness he'd ever known. He said, "The fact that the two of you are here today sitting in my office tells me so much about you both and your faith."

Dr. Beckham told us about Dr. Romano, who had recently moved her practice in with his. With her many degrees, she is far above a simple nutritionist. Dr. Beckham felt she could explain the specifics of fibromyalgia and, more importantly, help us both understand the disease and the role nutrition plays in it. People from all over the world fly in to see her, so it was unlikely she would have time to see us, but he said he'd try, even if he had to beg for just a few moments.

He came back after a few minutes and said, "Okay, I've got you ten minutes," during which, we found out later, she'd planned to eat her lunch.

Dr. Beckham sent us back to the waiting room to wait for Dr. Romano's assistant, Melody, to call us back.

Instead of calling us, Melody walked out and said, "I want the two of you to drive down the street a couple of blocks. Turn left and then turn right. There's this nice little restaurant that serves gluten-free food you'll love. Be back here by two o'clock. Dr. Romano has had a cancellation."

We knew God had worked that out in his wonderful way. But we didn't know until later that even Melody was shocked by the cancellation. The next time we saw her, she said, "Do you know it's so rare that Dr. Romano has cancellations, that after you left, I took the time to go back through her books. She has not had a two-hour cancellation in over five years." Yet she'd had one that day while we were sitting in the office, talking to Dr. Beckham.

Framed doctorates and degrees hung all around the walls in Dr. Romano's comfortable and inviting office. I've never seen so many.

Steve said he'd never seen so many. They were from institutions and teaching hospitals throughout the world.

Dr. Romano welcomed us with a friendly handshake along with a smile, which lit up her beautiful face. I immediately felt like I'd been welcomed into a shelter or respite from our never-ending storm by this kind, sweet, and energetic lady. Who would have known she, herself, had spent many years of her life paralyzed in a wheelchair with no hope of recovering.

She had my file, which was over two inches thick, sitting on her lap. Those were my records I'd been sending to Dr. Beckham since the phone consultations started with him two years before. After greeting us and discussing what our marriage had been through, she turned her attention to Steve. He was sitting in a desk chair on rollers. She turned his chair, pulling it toward her, saying, "I know why you're here. It's okay, I understand. First of all, I want you to know I refuse to see a married patient who has fibromyalgia unless their spouse is with them. Your wife, as well as many other patients of mine, has had to deal with this awful disease that no one understands, for the most part alone."

As Steve listened attentively, she continued, "I've looked through her file, and I want you to know that it's a miracle your wife is sitting right here in this chair in my office today. She should be dead. Everything I'm seeing in her blood work tells me the fibromyalgia has been there all along. Doctors are just not trained to look for what I'm trained to look for."

Shocked by what she'd said, Steve looked at me with huge eyes filled with tears. He didn't say anything then.

Dr. Romano continued, "It's your wife's research that has kept her alive. The fact is that when she didn't get any help and no one believed her, she didn't give up. She got on a computer, read books, and pursued a diagnosis that quite literally saved her life."

She then picked up the pretty heavy bag of supplements that I carried with me that day and told Steve that I had figured out myself what I could and couldn't take to keep going. Then she said something that totally shocked Steve.

"If the disease hadn't killed her, because it could've since she also has celiac, she stood a pretty good chance of taking her own life."

That's when Steve looked at me with horror. "You wouldn't have done that! My wife wouldn't have done that! You wouldn't have done that, would you?"

By then my tears were flowing. "Yes, I could have easily done that," I timidly said. "Of course I thought about it on many occasions. When the pain got so bad, and there were no medical answers for what I had, it was easy to lose all hope. And when I didn't feel you believed that I was really sick—you, of all people, the one person in this world that should have believed—yes, I thought about doing that. Then I would think of you, our children, and our God. No matter how badly I suffered, I couldn't impose that much pain and suffering on each of you. So all I could do was to continue to pray for the right doctor who would finally diagnose what was wrong."

We both cried many tears that day.

Dr. Romano spent two hours with us, went through every bottle, and told me which ones were right for my body and which ones weren't. Each time she put a bottle in the stack for me to discard, the more panicky I grew. I had finally sort of worked out a regimen that at least kept me out of bed and functional most days.

I walked out of her office with twelve to fifteen new bottles of supplements, and she didn't say start one at a time. She wanted me to start all the new supplements when I awoke the next morning. The most important thing I walked away with that day was her assurance that I would be well. I'd been sick for so long irreparable damage had already been done to my muscles, but despite that, for the first time in my life, I heard the word cure.

I gathered my courage and said, "You don't understand. I was starting to feel well enough that I even took a chance and made reservations three months ago for our whole family to go to Hilton Head. I wasn't sure at the time I'd be able to go. It might take four days to get down there. We might have to stop and spend the night, but that trip is coming up at the end of May and this is the end of April. You don't understand what supplements can do to me if I take the wrong thing."

"I do understand," she said. "Trust me. You'll go on that trip and feel like a different person."

I didn't know at the time, and only found out on my second or third visit with her, that she was very concerned about me. She had never before, in all her years of practice, changed every supplement all at one time. She was afraid for me; she was afraid of the way I looked in her office, and she knew it was necessary. In fact, being the strong Christian that she is, she sat up that night, all night, praying for me.

That miraculous visit was so encouraging, but the next morning I woke up to all those bottles lined up on the counter and didn't know what to take. I had her list: take this one for breakfast and then take another half for supper, take this one at lunch, this one at bedtime. But all I could do was stand there. I cried and cried. I couldn't handle it. I couldn't figure out what to take.

Steve had changed. He was a different man, one who loved, cared for, and supported me. He came up behind me. "Honey, I will help you. Don't worry."

We spent two hours trying to figure out what I was supposed to take before we ever thought about fixing breakfast. Then I sat there with this huge handful of pills in my hand. Now since that time,

Dr. Romano has reduced the medicines and supplements I take each morning. But still, when I lay them out, they total seventeen pills just to take with breakfast. Then there are the lunch, supper, and bedtime supplements. Some are huge pills, and I never have been able to swallow a pill that large before. They would always get stuck in my throat. I looked at those pills, knowing I couldn't swallow them.

At first, we tried breaking the tablets in half, but then I realized that if I took them while eating, one pill at a time between bites and with food washing it down, it wouldn't get stuck in my throat.

Steve became attentive in ways he'd never been before, and not just with the medicine. He slept with his arm wrapped around me tightly each night. If I rolled over, he rolled over with me. If I got up to go to the bathroom, he was immediately awake, asking, "Are you okay? Be careful. Don't fall."

Our next visit with Dr. Romano was in Greenville, South Carolina, a half hour from our home, where she saw patients monthly. Again, she reviewed my medicine and supplements and made adjustments. Dr. Beckham had already made major changes in my diet based on his own testing and knowledge of celiac and fibromyalgia, but she went a step further.

Dr. Romano did extensive blood work and tweaked everything from the specific brands of supplements I took, such as replacing the malic acid in Fibro-Care with Calcitrate since it has a greater amount of malic acid. She made several replacements to increase my magnesium, calcium, and other minerals to eliminate as much extra iron as possible due to my positive porphyria test results. In fact, even the jewelry I wear can only be made from platinum or gold made in specific countries. I couldn't cook with iron frying pans. I was using a magnesium spray on my muscles, and Dr. Romano suggested I add a scent-free sports cream with an analgesic in it over the magnesium sprayed area to feed the nerves going up and down my legs.

Even though it took a while, these suggestions and adjustments in my diet, medication, and supplements began to make a real difference in the way I felt and functioned. For the first time in more years than I could remember, I had days where I felt well physically. This, in turn, brought positive changes in my psychological outlook. The depression I'd battled for so long began to lift. It had been a long journey through hardships and despair, and I wasn't completely there yet, but the progress I'd made was tremendous. We got to take our trip to Hilton Head with our family. It was so nice as all ten of us went on a vacation together for the first time. That trip meant so much; it was filled with memories I'll always cherish.

Yet the underlying current was always Steve's infidelity. I had demanded details when I first found out, and now these haunted me. There were triggers in the most unexpected places, which filled me with sorrow and anger. We continued to see our therapists to work on our marriage as we still continued to cycle through good and bad days. And yet, God was steadfast during these weeks and months. Through His faithfulness and our hard work, our good days soon outnumbered the bad ones.

One of the casualties of my discovery of the infidelity was my work. For a year and a half, I was unable to work. When I sat at my computer, all I could think of was the e-mails I'd read. These thoughts and memories paralyzed me. I'd sit, think, and obsess; I couldn't leave those memories in the past. Everything I'd worked so hard to accomplish came to almost a standstill, and I really didn't care. I wasn't eating much at all and lost another forty pounds in a few short months.

My assistant, Shirley, came three mornings a week for about four hours. There were still orders to fill, and she made a few extra wreaths to list for sale in my Etsy shop. She would make the wreaths in my studio, take photos, and bring me the camera. The only thing I did concerning work during that time was process the photos, slowly, and list a few wreaths. I was in no hurry. I really didn't care about them—if they sold or not, or if they were listed or not.

Amazingly, during this time, even with everything else going on, Steve and I were growing closer. We had immediately begun praying together morning and night as we did devotionals as a couple. He was determined and intent on going out of his way to love me—to check on me, to call me from work, and even to pray for me over the phone when I was having a particularly bad day. We exchanged daily e-mails of prayer as we continued to pray for and lift each other up.

As time went on and my physical health improved, I walked across the breezeway to my studio to watch and chat with Shirley who was there, but I didn't make any wreaths. It was strange, like I was in mourning. My feelings were hurt, my heart ached, and yet, my body was improving. I still had no desire to do any form of work.

During that year and a half, when Steve was at home, my time was spent with him. We read uplifting, inspirational books together. We went on vacations together and learned things about each other's childhoods. We discovered secrets about each other and really got reintroduced again as best friends and husband and wife.

While getting to know each other like we never had before, we also learned how to walk with God. We were cultivating a very special relationship with Him and His will for our lives. God had His arms around us as He drew us closer together each and every day.

*Delight yourself also in the Lord, and He shall give you
the desires of your heart. Commit your way to the Lord,
trust also in Him, and He shall bring it to pass.*

PSALM 37:4-5 NKJV

Every now and then, I would try to work. I'd think I should send out a newsletter and sit down at the computer, but nothing would come. Before all this happened, I had filmed more instructional videos than ever before or since in a very short period of time. That had been a particularly inspired time in my life as I came up with ideas, following through with them quickly and with no hesitation. I worked hard and was excited about the direction my business was going. This inspiration along with my unending ideas turned into products that sold very quickly.

But in this time, that desire and those inspiring thoughts and feelings had left me. My heart was turning toward more important thoughts and desires.

I worked on growing closer to my husband. That was first and foremost in my mind. I still didn't care about the business. It was just a thing—granted, a thing that had meant a lot to me in the past, a thing born from a talent that God had given to me, but still just a thing. My business wasn't nearly as important as growing closer to my husband, being able to learn to forgive, and to nurture and grow the kind of marriage God wants us to have, the one He talks about in His Word.

I was suddenly married to a totally different man, one who treated me with such respect, love, and sincere care. At times, I would think: *Where is he? Where is the man I was married to? He couldn't just disappear totally or change that much, could he?*

He did, and he had.

As I grew stronger mentally, I grew even stronger physically. As days, weeks, and months flew by, my desire to work again peeked through as my heart healed.

I will never forget the very first newsletter I sent out after eighteen months. The headline was "Nancy's Back …" The open rate on that newsletter was more than any online business could ever hope to have. Virtually everyone who opened that newsletter sent me a message saying they'd missed me and had been worried about me. I had received e-mails, messages from customers, and comments on my website for the entire eighteen months. I had ignored these messages during that year and a half, but then I began to respond back to a few at a time.

Much hard work still lay ahead in all areas of our lives, but God's grace strengthened me and us. The tough times I'd been through hardened my resolve to make up for the lost years on all fronts. I had felt God was silent so many times, but now I realized He was, in fact, right there carrying me and protecting me, even in the lowest moments. Like a beautiful tapestry painstakingly woven over time, my life had become an amazing portrait of what God had willed it to be. I can honestly say now I wouldn't trade it for anything.

Do I still have my low moments and periods of illness? Sure. But now I know how to identify the causes and correct them. My journey through fibromyalgia took decades. The lessons I learned I'm now passing on to others—the hundreds of people who've e-mailed me with similar stories, people I've met at conferences or conventions, and the ones who happen upon this book because they're searching for solutions to their own health issues. I pray that something I've written will inspire them to never give up until they find their own path to wellness.

Chapter Fourteen

But they that wait upon the Lord shall renew [their] strength;
they shall mount up with wings as eagles; they shall run,
and not be weary; [and] they shall walk, and not faint.

ISAIAH 40:31

Given that I did so little for a year and a half where Ladybug Wreaths was concerned, I'm shocked the business survived. I often ask myself, *How did it survive? How could it survive?* Not only did it survive, but like a beautiful tree during a harsh winter, it quietly and steadily flourished as its roots spread, seeking nourishment—nourishment it wasn't getting from me.

The business I planted took on a life of its own when I couldn't tend it; like that tree, it continued to grow larger, bit by bit and stronger, one customer at a time. Like that tree in the wintertime, customers saw its buds as a promise of beautiful things to come.

God was not only nurturing my marriage, but he was also quietly nurturing a business he created through me and my talents. A business for my entire life—a business with as firm a foundation as our faith and our marriage had now.

If I had lost the business during those eighteen months, that would have been fine with me. I had also learned many lessons, where I'd failed as a wife and what my husband needed and desired from me. What mattered most was growing closer to Steve, devoting all my energy to the marriage God intended for us. But God had other plans in mind for us as husband and wife. He also had other plans for us to grow and nurture a business that would reach hundreds and thousands of women who were and are facing some of the same trials as we did.

I started back to work slowly, careful not to damage what we were rebuilding and recreating. "Nancy's Back …" was talked about in groups on Facebook, by my newsletter list, and by people who knew me that I didn't even know. Very few asked where I had been or what had happened. They just accepted me as I was: someone who loved, cared, and understood them. It was as if we all merely turned a page, a chapter in our lives and reconnected.

After that first newsletter in eighteen months, my business began growing and changing very quickly. Ladies anxiously looked for new and exciting how-to videos that would teach them to do something with their own two hands that could possibly change their lives forever.

During these last few years, things have moved at an even quicker pace for Ladybug Wreaths, and we've created other online businesses. I have been busy working on and creating many new products from the ideas that are always flying around in my head. Now my personal coach and Internet guru Jim Cockrum, calls Steve and me, full of many more ideas to grow and expand my business, which seems to be growing and changing all by itself. Jim has been instrumental in growing my business, but more important, he was a great friend to Steve and me throughout our marriage crisis.

I have filmed so many instructional DVDs on wreath design; I can't keep up with a current count as to how many. Let's just say they number in the hundreds. There are free videos found on my website, *LadybugWreaths.com*, my community/membership site,

NancysInnerCircle.com and my YouTube Channel, *YouTube.com/LadybugWreaths*. To my amazement, the views on my YouTube Channel have now grown to over three and a half million views.

Over a dozen videos on DVD are sold on my website, Amazon, and Etsy. Many more downloadable instructional videos are sold on my websites as well.

As I gained more confidence in myself and my abilities, I began hosting wreath-making workshops in my home for ladies wanting to grow their businesses very quickly. They also wanted to know all about my illness and what I did to keep it under control.

These workshops are such a hit and so much fun. After spending a day—or sometimes two days—teaching, my heart swells as these ladies tell me good-bye with smiles, hugs, and excitement as they return home with knowledge and skills to help build a flourishing and profitable business just as Sharon Royer below did.

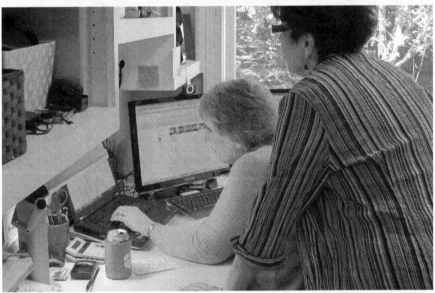

I received e-mails daily from ladies desperately wanting help as they were fighting their own debilitating illness. I pointed out the importance of finding the right doctor and eating the right foods. I was always aware that many, just like me, had no self-confidence and a very poor self-image while fighting battles that attacked them daily.

My community/membership site, Best of Nancy, has now grown into Nancy's Inner Circle with numbers of subscribers increasing daily. Like the other resources I'd established, this helped people take their first steps in starting their own businesses. We had begun reaching more and more women dealing with many of the same problems as me. Jim was excited that I was now able to reach out to others in hopes of making a difference in their lives, so he e-mailed me one day to ask a very important question.

Hi Nancy, I would like for you to come to Orlando and present your story at my Conference.

To understand why I was so overwhelmed with this question, you need to know a little more about Jim. His credentials show him as the most trusted Internet marketer online today. In addition, he is a radio host on Silent Sales Machine Radio, and author of *Silent Sales Machine* and *Free Marketing 101*. But all of that means nothing unless you know the heart of this humble, giving Christian man as we have come to know him.

This overwhelming question changed the direction of my business, not to mention my own self-image and personal growth. And, best of all, I was now able to share this with the man of my dreams, my husband, Steve.

Hmm… I reread and then closed Jim's e-mail. Wow, what an honor, I thought, but I ignored the invitation, going on about my busy schedule. I found myself wondering if Jim really understood what he was asking and how hard this would be for me. All the years I'd been sick, there was also the panic attacks and anxiety I had to deal with. I'd respond to Jim another day, since there was absolutely no way this was something I could do.

A few days later, another e-mail appeared. The subject line was: *Nancy, did you see this?* I thought to myself, *Well, of course, Jim, I saw that. How could I miss it? But I can't stand up in front of a crowd of 125 people for ten minutes telling my story*. At least, that's what I believed Jim was asking of me at that time.

Accepting Jim's offer would definitely be out of my comfort zone; not even that—more like impossible for me. Actually getting on a plane was out of my comfort zone. I had been through a lot. I couldn't get up in front of a crowd of my peers and completely fall apart, could I? These days, each step forward was with God and my devoted, loving husband at my side.

But I knew this time I had to respond. Jim had done so much to help me grow my business. He discovered me years before from a short e-mail reply thanking him for a suggestion he made in his e-book *Silent Sales Machine*. Did I mention what a huge difference that suggestion made in the growth and sales of my online business?

Jim had called me from time to time offering his expert advice, wisdom, and much-needed encouragement. His coaching opened my eyes to an Internet business and presence I would have never dreamed of. He continues to open doors that lead to more growth and success.

Once I even received a call from Jim saying: "God told me to call you today, and I always do what I'm told. How are you?" Little did he know that when God told him to call, it was at a time when Steve and I were going through a very difficult situation.

So as I quietly reflected upon the two e-mails I'd received, having known for some time that God was guiding my steps, I suddenly realized I needed to respond to Jim's invitation. The choice was mine. I had been given a unique opportunity not many get to experience. I could fail—fall flat on my face—or I could encourage and inspire others to reach their dreams and goals like I was doing.

When I finally responded to the invitation asking me to come to Orlando and present my story, little did I know how it would change the direction of my business, not to mention the positive boost it would give to my own self-image and personal growth. By taking action and giving my best to Jim and the conference, there are no words to describe what I received back.

This had become another chance to encourage and inspire others to reach their dreams and goals. Although I knew this was a trip I should make, and that it was truly God's will that I tell my story, I couldn't help but think that when it really came down to it, I wouldn't go; something unexpected would happen again in my life, causing me not to be able to make it. After all, that's the way it had been for me most of my life. What made me think this trip would be any different?

Nevertheless, I said yes, so the preparations began. First on the agenda were flight and hotel reservations. If you have a chronic illness like fibromyalgia, you know these types of preparations are not so easy. You can't do it the normal way by going online and booking a round-trip flight within minutes. There are special preparations and services you have to plan for and schedule. You have to talk to employees (more than one), making sure your requests are duly noted and followed through. You also have to call at least two more times to make sure everything is in place. Only then can you be confident there will be no glitches that will affect you and your body much more than most normal travelers.

I had to ensure wheelchairs were available to assist me in getting to the gate on time, with another waiting for me when our flight landed. My long lists of questions were finally answered to my satisfaction. But that was just the beginning …

Even though my fibromyalgia was in a better state of remission than ever before, I still had to sleep in a soft bed or I would wake up with a stiff back and a lot of pain. Next began the calls to the hotel. "Do your mattresses have a pillow top?" I asked. "Well, if you don't know, can you please send someone to check out the room for me by sitting on the bed?"

"Okay, we checked," they reported. "The beds feel pretty firm to us. Maybe you need to make further arrangements."

Through trial and error, Steve and I knew we could do that—it would just take a little more planning, but if this had come up years ago, I would have stayed home and slipped into a deep depression. We started searching for a single-size three-inch bed topper, and then a large suitcase that could contain the tightly rolled mattress that jumps out like a jack-in-the-box when the suitcase is opened. Oh, and then, there's the extra $35.00 fee to check that extra large, heavy bag, but … that's okay. We would do whatever was necessary to get there and assure that we enjoyed the trip.

Looking back on this now, it really seems funny! Oh, and I haven't even gotten to the other questions I had of the hotel staff such as: "How large is your hotel?"

This one threw me off a little when they answered, "It is very large. We are wrapped around one of the largest shopping malls in Orlando."

Instead of being pleased—how most other women would react upon hearing they'll be adjacent to a huge mall—I'm thinking, *Uh-oh, that's not good. How will I get around? How far will I have to walk? Can I really do this? Do they have a wheelchair or a scooter?*

Granted, I might have been making this harder and more complicated than need be, but for me to travel, I needed and wanted the security of knowing exactly what awaited. It's always been the unknown that gets me in trouble. Surprises throw me off. My body then reacts with stress. And stress, in turn, would always make fibromyalgia worse. What's more, I hadn't even gotten to the questions about gluten-free restaurants and where they were located.

The day finally came for us to leave. I was actually doing it! We were packed and in the car on our way to the airport. The extensive preparations had overshadowed my speech, which I should have been practicing daily. But thanks to my dear friend Linda, I had a nice PowerPoint presentation with photos to show on the large screen as I spoke. I had my notes typed word for word in case I panicked or got tongue tied and didn't have a clue what to say.

All of these extra preparations made this a very expensive trip for us. Steve was so sweet and kind. He never complained one bit. He was proud of me; he was so excited to be going on a trip with his wife, the business person, to present at a very important conference. We had missed out on so much during the long years of my illness. To be stepping out and doing something like this was an awesome experience for us both—a dream come true.

The trip was a whirlwind of excitement. Calls, e-mails, and texts had started coming in several weeks beforehand, setting up lunch dates, dinner dates, meetings, and all sorts of networking opportunities. I was asked by people I had only heard of to meet for lunch or to talk about business opportunities. I now know what a "power breakfast" is, and I love it!

I couldn't get over the fact that these experts wanted to meet and talk to me—that they even knew who I was. I was surprised when I realized I had a name that other successful entrepreneurs recognized. I found out later there were women and men who attended that particular conference, not only because they wanted to meet and learn from Jim, but because they heard I would be telling the story of my life.

Our first night was very special as we sneaked away from the hotel to enjoy dinner with Jim and his wife, Andrea Cockrum, Jim's mother, his assistant, and my friend Linda. To be able to have such a special time together with this awesome family and team meant so much to us both.

When I gave my presentation that weekend, I conquered a fear that had been with me my entire life. My heart pounded, my breath caught in my throat, and my stomach churned. I went to the restroom several times before it was my turn, and on my last trip I prayed to my God, knowing He would give me strength and courage exactly when I needed it, not necessarily before. And He did.

As I looked out at the crowd of over 350 smiling faces, I had to smile too. I think I might have even giggled as I realized, *I'm here! Okay, Lord, let's do it.*

I spoke of my life, my illness, and my business—for over an hour. Steve moved around the large meeting room with a smile on his face and a camera in hand, making sure not to miss a single shot from every angle. Men in the audience wiped tears away. I saw the looks on many faces. I knew I had made the right choice to follow God's leading to be in that room at that moment. He gave me an overabundance of strength, yet I leaned on Him the entire time. And, I rarely glanced at all those precisely written notes. I really didn't need them.

Upon finishing, I received a standing ovation. Of all the people who spoke that weekend, I was the only one who received a standing ovation. Tears flowed as people I admire—very successful entrepreneurs—stood in line to talk to me; they congratulated me and shared their own stories of pain and wanting to overcome. I had done it! I had overcome. My business changed that day; my life changed that day. That began a series of changes in my life and our businesses that still continue to this day—a business that has been in God's plan for us all along.

I've learned that confidence and strength may not always be with me beforehand, but at the exact moment I need them, God will provide. I know that beyond a shadow of a doubt now. At any point in my journey, He gives me exactly what I need, exactly when it is needed. I am learning to trust and have faith. If only I had felt that many years before when I thought God had deserted me.

And my God will supply every need of yours
according to his riches in glory in Christ Jesus.
PHILIPPIANS 4:19 ESV

I now have a loyal following of women and men who look to me for encouragement and to hear the words I say to them so often: "You CAN do it, I know YOU can!"

Ladybug Wreaths (*www.LadybugWreaths.com*) sends out a newsletter each week to over twelve thousand people. I design door wreaths and sell them through my Etsy shop. I've sold thousands of beautiful wreaths that are shipped to celebrities and customers all over the world.

My Facebook business page has around thirty thousand "likes" and followers. "Nancy's Inner Circle" is a membership site for my community filled with hundreds of women fighting problems just as I have for so many years. They want and need a reason to get out of bed every day. They need something they can do with their own two hands. They need to be able to find their God-given talents and use them in such a way that glorifies Him while bringing in much needed extra income to help pay for their overwhelming medical bills.

I have written seven Kindle books and published a half dozen instructional books, which are sold on Amazon. *Sourcing Power* rose to the top and became a Kindle Best Seller in only two days. My best-selling e-book *My Secret Vendors* was Jim Cockrum's idea, one that didn't go over well with me at first. Jim was persistent, and there have now been five rewrites since October of 2010, bringing in a substantial income as they continually sell.

My last book was finished in 2016, *Make Your Own Wreaths: For Any Occasion in Any Season* with Stackpole Publishers. They contracted me to write a book about how to make "wild & woodsy" natural wreaths. It took over six sessions with an awesome photographer to take over four thousand photos, which were then carefully chosen for use in my new book.

Jesus is in control. He has taken "Beautifully Broken Me" and used me to make a difference in the lives of *so* many. He is in control of my business as it expands in many directions at once. I could not begin to do any of this on my own but only through God's guidance with the people He places in my path to coach, inspire, and encourage me. Then I in turn coach, inspire, and encourage others.

I can do all things through Christ who strengthens me.

PHILIPPIANS 4:13 NKJV

I don't know what plans God has for my business from here on. What I do know is that whatever those plans are, I will follow Him with a heart full of wonder and blessings, enjoying every step of the way! My friend Molly Alexander wrote,

By picking up the pieces of a broken life and putting them back together, a person cannot help but be changed. This change is a beautiful thing resulting in a deeper understanding of others and their situations, and giving us a chance to share our experiences with them, showing them that there is a way out—a light at the end of the tunnel ... I believe that I have not just been broken, but put back together by God in a beautiful way—a way that I could have never imagined on own.

The above statement is what I believe God has done in my life so I can show you a light at the end of the tunnel in yours.

Chapter Fifteen

You are in God's light when you are creating.
Food is critical, so when you eat, make it count.

DR. ROMANO, *nutritionist*

Everyone wants to know what I can eat. I get questions and e-mails all the time. What can you eat? How did you do it? How in the world did you lose over 110 pounds?

First, I want to reiterate that although this has worked for me, I cannot guarantee scientifically or medically that it will work for you. Do the research, as I did, and you will find many studies to back up what I'm sharing here.

At first this new way of eating was hard. I thought I could not do it. I wondered what I would be able to eat. It seemed like nothing! That's what I thought and it's probably what you're thinking too. But discovering what foods I could and couldn't eat has changed my life. God has changed my life through my new "healthy" lifestyle and through the marvelous doctors my husband and I found who knew immediately what was killing me and the immediate and major changes I needed to make in the foods I ate.

But, thank you, Lord! Now I'm healthy, and I'm flourishing at the "tender" age of sixty-six, feeling better than I have felt since I was twenty-nine years old! And it's all because of what I eat and the supplements I take (but this chapter will deal only with my diet).

It's easier to talk about foods that I *cannot* eat, namely ones that contain gluten, lactose, or soy. As a part of my diet, I eat no gluten, which is found in wheat flour, or any whole grains (except brown rice).

First of all, I want to make it clear that wheat hasn't always been bad for our bodies. I'm sure you're wondering, as I did, why people didn't suffer with fibromyalgia many years ago. And, it wasn't just because they didn't recognize fibromyalgia then—and not because people were sick with it and were not being diagnosed.

The reason our bodies cannot tolerate gluten (wheat) now in our diets is that it is not the same wheat that our ancestors grew, ground, and ate. It has been genetically modified (GMO) and has been changed into something that our bodies cannot tolerate, and conversely cannot be considered nourishment when digested.

If you have fibromyalgia, or even think you have this, try eating as healthy, natural, and organically as possible. Fibromyalgia was not a disease or even a problem one hundred years ago. Do you know why? They didn't have all of these chemicals, preservatives, and insecticides in their foods then. A good rule of thumb is, if you couldn't find that food a hundred years ago … then don't eat it now! Simple, huh?

Eating right proves to be a difficult task for many. There are about thirty thousand genetically modified food products on US grocery store shelves. These are the top-nine genetically altered foods (and I cannot have any of them): soy, cottonseed, corn, canola oil, alfalfa, cow's milk, aspartame, US papaya, and sugar beets.[5]

Over the past decade, biotech companies like Monsanto have dominated dinner tables with crops like corn, soybeans, and canola modified to survive lethal doses of herbicides, resulting in increased herbicide use, a surge in herbicide-resistant weeds, and the contamination of organic and conventional crops.[6] According to the Center for Food Safety, more than half of all processed food in US grocery stores—items like cereals, corn dogs, and cookies—contain genetically engineered (GE) ingredients.[7]

"This technology is a one-trick pony," says George Kimbrell, an attorney at the Center for Food Safety. "They don't help us feed the world, they don't fight climate change, and they don't help us better the environment. They just increase pesticides and herbicides. That's what they do."[8]

Currently, 85 percent of GE crops are designed to resist herbicides. Companies like Syngenta, Bayer, and Dow have all created their own herbicide-tolerant seeds, modified to withstand the company's corresponding herbicide treatment. But it's Monsanto, the world leader in GE seed production that has benefited the most from biotechnology by packaging its Roundup Ready line of GE seeds with its Roundup herbicide. Monsanto, whose roots began in creating toxic chemical concoctions like polychlorinated biphenyls (PCBs) and DDT, is now the world's leading producer of glyphosate, the active ingredient in Roundup herbicide.[9]

What on Earth Can You Eat?

So you might be thinking—what can you eat?

I do eat bread every day, but it is bread I make in my $10.00-yard sale bread machine. I use Pamela's bread mix, which is made from rice flour. I buy this from Amazon and make it a couple of days a week—because my husband is now wheat-free also. (His arthritis got better when he left off wheat.) I eat pasta, macaroni, spaghetti, etc. made from rice flour also. If you were to come to dinner at my house, you would not know you were eating gluten-free! We can eat pizza, which I make using Kinnikinnick or Udi's brand gluten-free pizza crust.

I can eat rice flour, almond flour, tapioca starch flour, and coconut flour. Sometimes, you see bread that says it doesn't have wheat, but many "ancient grains." Well, that one fooled me for a while and I ate a few slices. Boy, it was yummy until I started getting sick and found that it also has gluten in it.

- Gluten is found in flour and oats.

- Gluten is also in the coatings of many medicines, pills, and supplements.

- Gluten can be found in different types of makeup (so I have started using Lancôme, and I don't seem to have any problems with it). There were many times when I tried new makeup and started feeling really badly—sometimes after a day, and sometimes after a week. Even after I knew I had celiac disease, it still was a long process trying to figure out why my body was reacting the way it was!

- Gluten is found as glue on the envelopes that you lick! I had always noticed that when I sealed an envelope, I felt bad, but didn't know why until I found this out!

- Gluten is used as filler in so many different meds—whether they are over the counter or prescribed.

- Many of the generic meds have minute fillers in them which are many times soy and/or gluten.

- My druggist has had to call the manufacturer for me more than once when I got sick as I was trying a generic drug. You see, they are not required to say it has gluten or soy in it unless it is over a certain percentage.

I have also found that I am just as allergic, if not more so, to soy. This really didn't show up until I had been off gluten for a month or so. I have found that there are many, many spices which have soy in them. As a matter of fact, there is so much that has soy in it, that I am totally amazed! Some examples of this are:

- Most salad dressings

- Lots of potato chips

- Many corn chips

- Most chocolate chips in a bag are coated in soy to keep them from sticking together, so when I purchased gluten-free chocolate chip cookies or muffins, I found they had soy in them. Therefore, I purchase the Enjoy Life chocolate chips as well as chocolate chip cookies, because they have no soy.

- A-1 Sauce, barbecue sauce, and most of the steak sauces have soy in them.

- Many pills have soy in the coatings and in the filler ingredients.

- Soy is also found in many spices. Some have so much soy that I am really surprised.

But that's okay. I truly can live without gluten and soy for the rest of my life—more than happy to, as a matter of fact! With some of these other foods, I sneak a little every now and then, and although I don't feel great afterwards, I am not deathly ill.

When I started this diet, I was also told that I needed to leave off all lactose or milk products. These include cow's milk, cheese, and yogurt, as well as whey, which are also found in many foods that you would never suspect they are in.

The need to go dairy-free came as no surprise. For most of my life, I had noticed every time I had cow's milk, my stomach would swell up as if I had eaten a watermelon.

- I loved salmon stew but couldn't eat much of it at all.

- I loved chicken 'n dumplings but couldn't eat much.

- I loved homemade ice cream but felt bloated after eating it too.

You know how they say you crave the things you're allergic to and cannot have? Well, I am a classic example of that. When I first started out, I didn't really know what gluten would do to me if I accidentally digested some. I even insisted that we get a toaster that had four slots. The two on the right were for gluten-free bread, and the slots on the left were for regular. I didn't even want crumbs of wheat bread to touch my gluten-free rice flour bread.

What About Eating Out?

Steve will be the first to tell you that in the beginning, I was afraid to go out to eat. Actually it was too risky, too serious, so I decided I'd rather stay home. I didn't know what to order, and then, I thought they wouldn't take me seriously, and I'd get really sick. This even applied to places that offered gluten-free menus also. I have found waiters and waitresses who would have to ask me what gluten was. That's when I felt like getting up and leaving that particular restaurant (and there were many times I did).

Through the years more and more places now offer gluten-free menus, and really know what that means. Olive Garden has gluten-free penne pasta with a tomato sauce which is yummy. Now we have a Mellow Mushroom pizza place here. They can prepare gluten-free dough and go so far as to cook their gluten-free pizzas in a separate oven from their other pizzas. When you order, they even ask if it is for an allergy because it is sort of becoming a trend now to eat gluten-free because many people have heard it is a healthier option.

Outback Steakhouse has gluten-free menus, and all their staff is trained to know exactly what that is. They are very cautious there!

If we are eating in a restaurant without a gluten-free menu:

- I first look for shrimp or scallops (if they have good ones), and I ask if they have a small frying pan to sauté them only in butter and a little salt. Red Lobster is good about doing this. (Nicer restaurants are more than happy to prepare food in a special way.)

- Then I order a baked potato with butter on the side.

- To that I add a salad—if I have remembered to bring my own salad dressing because I know it does not have soy in it. I have also learned that I can eat a salad without dressing at all. I ask for extra tomatoes, and that sort of makes up for no dressing. There is always the option of olive oil and vinegar, but vinegar seems to cause problems for me if I add too much, so I tend to just stay away from it.

- Otherwise, I ask if they have steamed vegetables with a little butter and salt—no spices.

If we are eating in a steakhouse that does not have a gluten-free menu:

- We go to Logan's steakhouse every Friday night with friends.

- They are the first restaurant I tried this with. And that is asking them to clean a section of the grill, and then cooking me a steak with only salt on it.

- The staff at Logan's knows me now and when they see me come in, we usually have a waiter/waitress who already knows my restrictions.

- But … there are still times (although few) where they slip up and bring me a steak where I can see the spices sitting on top of it, and I have to return it to the kitchen. Again, I am so particular about spices because most of them contain soy.

I have to remain cautious all the time when I go out to eat, but that does not stop me from going out anymore. I just keep my eyes open and am very aware.

Steve has missed eating at quick fast-food places like Subway, Kentucky Fried Chicken, and so many more. I used to miss them, too, but I knew I just could not take a chance to even go in those places even if they served salad. I can honestly say now that I have no desire any more to frequent any of these types of fast-food restaurants.

Sample Meals

Breakfast

- 1 egg, scrambled
- 1 slice gluten-free toast (Pamela's Bread Mix, with many other options available)
- 16 ounces of water

Lunch

- Sandwich with a piece of Pamela's bread cut in half with mustard (never mayonnaise)
- Sliced turkey or sliced ham (Make sure it does not have many preservatives. I have found a brand in the grocery store that does not seem to bother me, so I stick with that. It is packaged in a container. The fresher sandwich meats that you have sliced always seem to affect me a little.)
- Baked potato chips with no preservatives (The ingredients on the bag say potatoes and salt only.)

- Salad with gluten-free/soy-free dressing filled with lots of greens, tomatoes, Baked potato (I wash a potato, wrap it with wet paper towels, and cook it in the microwave for about six or seven minutes with a cover over it, which keeps it soft and it doesn't dry out. I put a little cheese and maybe a little broccoli on it, if I have some, and a little butter.)

- The next day, I will eat the other half of the turkey burger that I had the night before at supper. It is lean turkey without any bread and one slice of American cheese. I add a little mustard and ketchup on top.

- My salad consists of: green-leaf lettuce, slivers of almonds, Craisins, a little finely grated parmesan cheese, salad tomatoes, leftover cooked broccoli, and maybe some fruit.

- Half of a baked chicken breast left over from last night
- Green beans cooked with cut-up potatoes on top
- Carrots cooked with just a little water and salt

Snacks

- This afternoon, I will probably eat some gluten-free crackers from the health food store with some peanut butter. At first I had to purchase "all natural" peanut butter, but now I can eat peanut butter from the health food store without much sugar added.

- Nuts such as almonds, cashews, or a few peanuts (Don't eat as many peanuts.)

- Any type of fruit (I like to cut up an apple, banana, and grapes into a bowl and keep it in the fridge to grab a bite when I want something sweet. I also enjoy cantaloupe.)

- Sliced ham

- Gluten-free Kinnikinnick chocolate chip muffin (Note: I couldn't eat these at first because they made me feel bad, but now I can since I have been on the diet for a while. I still would probably feel better not eating them, because chocolate chips are dusted with a powder that keeps them from sticking together and this powder has trace amounts of gluten in it.)

- There are also gluten-free snacks available. Just be careful with these and not eat too many of them. They can raise your cholesterol and not be really healthy at all.

My Favorite "Safe" Foods

Chicken

- Chicken boiled in water or chicken broth (We also love roasted chicken cooked with olive oil, Jane's Krazy Mixed-Up Salt, and coated in almond or coconut flour.)

- Chicken strips cooked in a frying pan with real butter, Krazy Salt, and paprika (This is very good!)

- Chicken baked in oven with Kraft Original barbecue sauce (Note: I have to be very careful with barbecue sauce, because most of it has soy or soybean oil in it—this one does not.)

Hamburger

- Hamburger patty cooked in frying pan with just a little extra virgin olive oil, a little water to keep it from drying out, and Krazy Salt

- I order hamburger patties in restaurants, specifying that I don't want bread. From time to time, they have mixed up my order and brought out a burger with bread on it, then suggested that they take it off. I tell them no, I cannot eat the burger after it has been on a bun; they have to cook me another, or they will have a sick customer.

- I stir-fry hamburger meat or turkey meat mixed with water until water is cooked out. Then, I add Rotel tomatoes (mild), a frozen bag of mixed vegetables, a little tomato juice and tomato sauce, and then mix it with leftover Uncle Ben's cooked rice. This is really good! We eat it in a bowl with a piece of toast.

Weight Loss: An Added Benefit of My Diet

What about the weight loss? Well, obviously I was overweight from being sick for so long. I didn't change my way of eating to lose weight. I changed my way of eating to be happy and healthy and to be able to enjoy my life and my family again. The weight loss was a plus—an amazing plus! I did love being a size eight petite, but I'm a little more than that now.

To sum it up, I now eat as healthy and natural as I can. My diet consists mainly of food that is organic, natural, fresh, home grown and/or bought at farmer's markets. This means: no gluten, no dairy products (milk with lactose, whey, cheese), no MSG, as little sugar as possible, no canned foods, no processed foods, etc.

Over the next few pages, I will show you some of the many delicious meals I've prepared.

Homeade chicken salad and fruit. Yummy!

Smoothie made with rice milk, protein powder, blueberries

Gluten-free pie crust with chocolate filling (rice milk)
and fresh cream. Yeah, I know—a *no-no!*

Plate prepared especially for me from Tupelo Honey restaurant. Baked chicken breast (no spices) and salad—green-leaf lettuce and fresh spinach, bacon, carrots, and feta cheese. Didn't eat their dressing. And, gluten-free toast. This was yummy!

My homemade chili with Pamela's gluten-free homemade bread.

Homemade meal with lots of fresh veggies and chicken—so good.

Quick meal at home: stir-fried squash & zucchini, cabbage, and sliced ham

Homemade gluten-free brownie, Cool Whip (I really shouldn't have), and a maraschino cherry. Yes, sometimes I do cheat a little on the dairy part, but nothing else!

For more information about foods I eat to help me feel better, please visit me on my personal blog site:
www.NancyAlexander.me

Epilogue

You turned my wailing into dancing; you removed my sackcloth and clothed me with joy, that my heart may sing to you and not be silent. O Lord my God, I will give you thanks forever.

PSALM 30:11-12

I am strong! I am courageous! I am an overcomer!

So are you!

You may have already known me before reading this book. You may have known about me because you were on my list and received newsletters from me each week. You could have purchased one or more of my how-to-make-a-wreath DVDs, downloadable videos, or e-books because you wanted to learn how to make beautiful wreaths for your door, or even to sell. Maybe you're one of thousands who follow me on Facebook; or maybe even one of millions who have viewed my videos on YouTube. Could you have possibly purchased from me the gorgeous wreath that might be hanging on your front door? Or, are you one of the very special ladies who have come to one of many workshops at my home? Maybe I caught your attention because you read where I have overcome some physical disabilities. I have grown a successful business and quite a faithful following while fighting a long and painful battle with fibromyalgia and celiac disease.

Many "About Me" pages are spread throughout the Internet: on websites, Facebook pages, Twitter, and more. Each version is a little different in some way, yet together they tell my story—or at least the version of the story I've let myself share up until now. You might have read my blog on NancyAlexander.me, or the one on LadybugWreaths.com. I have written many posts in various other venues that delve more into the personal side of my life.

You could have been at Jim Cockrum's CES conference in Orlando, Florida, in 2013, as God gave me, the shy, withdrawn woman who had always lacked self-esteem, the strength through His Spirit to speak in front of 350 people.

So now you have read this book, *My Journey Through Fibromyalgia: Rumors, Ravages, & the Rescue.* You have experienced my deepest, most personal fears, pain, and joy. Maybe you have shed a few tears with me as we have walked through the journey of my life together.

I was always so good at hiding when feeling not quite good enough, or like I didn't belong. I felt ashamed because I couldn't snap out of my illness, but I was also careful to make sure no one else could see that.

You may have been startled by revelations I shared with you. I want you to know these are revelations Steve and I have prayerfully shared with you together. It's my prayer your heart is filled with understanding as well as forgiveness for those who suffer chronic illnesses and their family members who might make poor choices because of their lack of understanding. It's my prayer that you have grown stronger in your faith after learning what happens when a debilitating illness strikes even the best of families.

As I began this book years ago, my mind was full of thoughts, ideas, and—yes—reluctance and confusion. You now know there were two stories. There was the public one that I decided to share with you as God laid a strong conviction on my heart to help and encourage you in your battle with whatever chronic illness, hurt, or problem may have knocked you down—the one you may now need strength in fighting to overcome.

But then there was the true, sometimes shocking behind-the-scenes story that, because of an even stronger conviction from God, Steve and I together decided needed to be told, although that was never our intention when this book was begun. We all deal with things in our lives we don't want to talk about. They may be embarrassing choices or bad decisions we're ashamed of.

What if …? Just what if …?

The struggles that we face from these decisions, battles that were meant to destroy us, can actually give us strength to find and fulfill God's purpose for our lives? These struggles, or setbacks, can help us move closer in our walk with God.

In the beginning, I was convinced that this painful underlying story should be kept quiet—buried and never discussed. I wanted to protect the ones I love, the ones closest to my heart. I believed this underlying story had no relevance pertaining to my story of "overcoming," since it was something so personal it could hurt those that I care about deeply, if not told properly.

As words filled pages and pages turned into chapters, Steve and I found ourselves having to make difficult and confusing decisions that were never anticipated. These decisions were whether to reveal certain circumstances or parts of our lives together to the world. We found ourselves thinking, *Which part of my story is this?* And finally, we came to the conclusion that they were both parts of the whole; the part I wanted to tell about how fibromyalgia had stolen my life and also the one I had decided not to tell but rather to hold deep within. The more I wrote the more Steve and I realized these circumstances were such an intermingled part of my battle of overcoming fibromyalgia that they had to be told together.

As I worked my way through words and feelings that filled many years, I was continually led back to one thought: *I am leaving off a very important thing. The one thing I knew I wouldn't have survived without God's help—our marriage!* You already had a sense of what my chronic illness did to me. But I then had to tell you what my chronic illness did to my husband, what a chronic illness, more often than you think, does to any spouse.

My thoughts immediately went back to e-mail after e-mail, mostly from women fighting chronic illnesses, especially fibromyalgia. A very important and similar thread runs through these e-mails. It leapt off those pages and into my mind and heart. Not only have these ladies confided in me that they had to fight outstanding odds in order to overcome, but they have, in many cases, had to fight this battle alone.

In Steve's and my marriage, as well as their marriages, at first there were hopes of help and healing with each new doctor visited and with each new med prescribed. This will be over soon, we all tell ourselves as days turn into weeks, weeks into months, and months into years. Oh, how I remember those weeks, months, and years so clearly. I remember telling myself, this will end soon. I was doing all I knew to do: praying to Jesus on a daily basis, pleading for His healing power.

In the hundreds and thousands of e-mails I have received, one statement jumps off the page to me each time. Their support person—their loved one or spouse—often isn't in the picture anymore. They've either given up or left to find a happier life they believe they deserve; or they've stayed, building walls that protect them and the lives they dream of having. My support person was and should have been my husband, Steve, as is the case for us all when we are fighting a battle for our health and our very lives. In God's plan, our spouse stands beside us because they have vowed before God to love and protect us; they stand beside us because it is the right thing to do, because it is necessary, or sometimes just because they have no other choice.

But since this can be so trying on the spouse of one with a chronic illness, in the latter case, they've become tired, worn out, and drained with nothing left to give. Caring for, loving, and supporting someone with a chronic illness is hard! Both parties learn how to turn feelings off or to put them on hold for their own sanity, their own protection. Hearts no longer feel the urgency and the overwhelming need for support. Satan, the deceiver, is doing his very best work in the midst of this pain, fear, and weakness.

His goal is to plant thoughts and questions in the minds of our loved ones. Questions about whether their spouses are really ill. Questions like: *Could she be using this so-called illness to control my life? How long is this going to continue? Will we ever have a normal life again? Will we be able to vacation as a family again? Will we have a happy family again like our friends do?* Oh, the deceiver is so good at planting these doubts and questions. The more he controls, the more his power grows within, taking over more and more thoughts and feelings to be his own. It becomes easier and easier for him to control more … and thus the downward spiral continues as it spins out of control.

The longer I struggled with pain while continuing to search for its cause, the more doctors we sought out. We both began feeling alone—strangers living in the same home. Many of you told me you had lost your spouse, that your marriage had not been strong enough to withstand the stress. Your husbands didn't believe you were really ill. They didn't understand the pain and despair you were going through each day.

That doesn't mean they didn't try; I know Steve tried. As we lay in bed night after night, I now know his desire to reach out and hold me was just as overwhelming as my desire to be held. I needed his strength, I needed his warmth, and most of all, I needed his love and his belief in me. Steve knew my body hurt so badly I could hardly bear to be touched. So we were strangers again—in our own bed.

Steve struggled with all that was going on, while the deceiver's attacks grew stronger and stronger within. Temptations were strategically placed, so Steve's thoughts and feelings were influenced more with each passing day, month, and year. After experiencing this pain, many husbands feel justified in leaving. They feel they have given all they had to give as they decide it's time to enjoy a happy life. Do you see what's happening here? A chronic illness is just as detrimental to the spouse as it is to the victim.

As we read in the Bible, the great deceiver prowls around looking for a crack in our armor. With a chronic illness to deal with in your home, there definitely is a crack, and it's not very hard to find. His never-ending mission to destroy the institution of marriage will yield results when he finds the tiniest of cracks, and we had a huge one.

Be alert and of sober mind. Your enemy the devil prowls around like a roaring lion looking for someone to devour.

1 PETER 5:8

Steve and I decided it was imperative that we share with you the entire story because it does have a happy ending. We have begun a new chapter in our lives—a new start with God at the head of our home. Our story has a fairy-tale ending. Our lives have been changed forever. I am treated like a queen and Steve is my knight in shining armor. I am loved and cherished beyond words. Every need is often met before I even realize it is a need.

When pain does come back, as it does from time to time, for I still battle fibromyalgia, I don't have to face it alone. I'll never have to face it alone again. I am prayed for and prayed over every single day—morning and night. There is a quiet understanding between my husband and me without words ever being spoken.

Steve holds onto me in bed as if he's afraid he'll lose the most precious gift he's ever been given. I'm awakened in the middle of the night by a pat on the head or a soft hand on my cheek just to make sure I'm still there. I feel him pulling the covers up underneath my chin and tucking them in around me, making sure I don't get chilled.

We lie in bed at night and talk and laugh until we fall asleep after praying for each child and thanking God for saving us. We awaken in the mornings to warm hugs, cuddles, smiles, and kisses. When Steve didn't have to get up early to go to work, we lay side by side planning our day and talking about God's will for our lives, for the lives of our children, and for my (now our) business. Now that Steve has retired, there are endless happy mornings just like this for us. This is such a special moment in our day as the morning sun streams in the window and across our faces, while making sunbeams dance on the wall.

We now have what God meant for us to experience all along in our marriage. Never in my wildest imaginings could I believe I would have experienced this in my lifetime. We now dance in the rain before daylight (yes ... really!) and jump in our car at midnight to catch the glimpse of a full moon from the top of a hill or to see a half dozen deer grazing across the meadow.

As we walk hand in hand into church on Sunday mornings, people stop us to comment about how happy we look. There is a glow on our faces as we look into each other's eyes with a knowing smile. We hold hands during the services—somehow bringing us closer to each other as well as to Jesus.

Your story can have a happy ending too. You can be loved, honored, and cherished so deeply that you know God is and will be the center of your life forever. You'll know He is the giver of the most awesome gift you'll ever experience in your lifetime. We had to give of our hearts; we had to trust in the only being that could have changed our lives: Jesus. We had to be willing to go through the pain of being drastically pruned so we could experience a renewal of springtime where our lives could grow and blossom together with joy and happiness.

If you're like we were, when experiencing such horrific pain, your first thought is to turn to those you think can help. We immediately did that. We turned to Christians who knew God's Word, we turned to those who loved Him and led their lives according to His purpose. But Steve and I knew no mere mortal could save us and save a marriage that was in such disrepair. Only our God, whom we believe in with all our hearts, could work to make the awful struggle in our lives work toward our good. When there was absolutely *no* other way to turn, and *no* other way out, we were left in such desperation that we knew Jesus was our only hope.

Do I blame my husband? Do I blame God? Of course I did while trying to deal with all the pain. We were in a pit with no way out; we were at the foot of a huge mountain of pain, hurt, and despair that loomed so huge in front of us that we lost sight of Jesus.

But now, there is no blame. We were both victims of horrific circumstances. There is forgiveness, which, to be honest, was hard. The Bible doesn't say forgiveness is easy. When I've needed God's forgiveness in my life, it was given freely without any questions. How could I not do for my husband what God does for me so freely?

In Mark 11:25 Jesus says, *"And when you stand praying, if you hold anything against anyone, forgive them, so that your Father in heaven may forgive you your sins."*

We are redeemed. We are two totally different people. I will always consider myself truly blessed to have married Stephen Danner Alexander, the man of my dreams, in 1972. I have told you this story—my story—so you will be watchful, keep your eyes open, and stand guard so as to not let your family go through what our family experienced.

Marriage is a sacred union; our love now proves it.

But every husband must love his wife as he loves himself,
and wives should respect their husbands.

EPHESIANS 5:33 GW

If onlys ... and what ifs ...

Many thoughts have gone through my mind while writing this book. While looking back at my life, there were many "if onlys," and "what ifs." I have experienced a deep desire to hear God talking to me. I hear others say they "heard a word from God," or He spoke to them. Oh, how I wanted that to be me—to know in my heart that my God would speak a word, His word to me as He told me which choice or decision was the right one; the one that was His will for me.

The more I've read and reread the words on these pages, the more I've dreamed of hearing His voice while living the story I've been writing about. Suddenly, I became so aware! I don't know how I've missed this before! I knew; I just knew ... God opened my heart and my mind as He reminded me how often I did hear His voice; how often he talked to me as He led me on the path to His perfect will for my life.

God had been speaking to me all along! Remembrances flash back into my consciousness ... as I remember words from Him that changed the path of my life.

There are words that led me to now be able to enjoy a happy life married to the man of my dreams. There are words He spoke that gave me the courage, and yes, sometimes even a push, to finish this book... my story. In my weakness, He was strong. The apostle Paul wrote, But He said to me, *"My grace is sufficient for you, for my power is made perfect in weakness." Therefore I will boast all the more gladly about my weaknesses, so that Christ's power may rest on me* (2 Corinthians 12:9).

Instead of abandoning me, Jesus was whispering: *"Come to me, all who are weary and heavy-laden, and I will give you rest"* (Matthew 11:28 NASB). It is my prayer that the words in this book can give you strength, determination, as well as an open heart to hear our God speaking to you.

God is always there. He is always on His throne. He's watching over us. He is always working for the good of those who love Him and have been called according to His purpose. He will reach down into lives and make them better when He sees you have lost control and don't know where to turn.

> *The Lord is close to the brokenhearted;*
> *he rescues those whose spirits are crushed.*
>
> PSALM 34:18 NLT

If you have marriage problems, turn to Jesus. He doesn't want to rebuild your marriage; He wants to restore it. Only Jesus can heal, only Jesus can save, only Jesus can restore—just as He did for us. That is why I wrote this book. This is why Steve and I wrote this book. That is why we want to share it with you.

Rejoice with us as we share with you how truly blessed we are.

Blessings, Nancy

About the Authors

While fighting the diseases of fibromyalgia and celiac for almost 40 years, **Nancy Alexander**, now a master wreath designer and teacher, found hope just when she thought there was none left. She discovered her God-given talent of creating unique wreaths. She has now sold many thousands of wreaths all over the world. An author of instructional and business books, Nancy's latest book, *Make Your Own Wreaths: For Any Occasion in Any Season* was published in July, 2016. Thousands of copies sold very quickly.

But, that wasn't all. Soon, this woman from Anderson, South Carolina, realized God's plans for her life were more than she could imagine. The path she walked, along with the illnesses that went undiagnosed for years, led her to ladies just like herself who desperately needed help.

Many lives have been changed through Nancy's sincere desire to help these ladies develop their own God-given gifts. She enjoys encouraging and teaching members of her private community, Nancy's Inner Circle: www.NancysInnerCircle.com.

Finding joy and hope restored in their lives again, these ladies love learning from Nancy.

Utilizing Nancy's many how-to books and videos, her students can create beautiful designs — giving them a reason to want to get out of bed each morning.

Nancy is grateful for the saving power of God as He leads her to help others fulfill their own dreams just as she has.

Nancy's other books can be accessed here:
www.NancyAlexanderBooks.com.

*L*aura Hodges Poole is a Christian writer with four books and dozens of articles, devotions, and short stories to her credit. All her books are available on Amazon.com. She is the 2016 *ACWC Badge of Honor* winner, 2014 *ACFW Genesis* semi-finalist, and 2012 *RWA Emily* finalist. Laura is also a non-fiction ghostwriter and collaborator. Her passion is encouraging others in their Christian walk through her blog, *A Word of Encouragement*. As an editor and member of The Christian PEN, Laura enjoys mentoring and helping other writers polish their work. Her upcoming Christian romance novel will be released in March 2018. When she's not writing, you might find her hiking, playing the piano, or being crafty. A mother of two, Laura lives in the upstate of South Carolina with her husband and son.

Notes

1   *Webster's Third New International Dictionary*, Unabridged, s.v. "fibromyalgia," http://unabridged.merriam-webster.com.

2   National Institute of Arthritis and Musculoskeletal and Skin Diseases, www.niams.nih.gov.

3   *Webster's Third New International Dictionary*, Unabridged, s.v. "celiac disease," http://unabridged.merriam-webster.com.

4   *Beautifully Broken Me: The Art and Musings of Molly Alexander,* http://beautifullybrokenme.blogspot.com.

5   Green America, http://action.greenamerica.org.

6   Earthjustice, http://earthjustice.org.m

7   Center for Food Safety, http://www.centerforfoodsafety.org.

8   *Down to Earth: Q&A with CFS Attorney George Kimbrell"* Earthjustice, http://earthjustice.org/features/ourwork/down-to-earth-qa-with-cfs-attorney-george-kimbrell.

9   *Monsanto's Chemical Romance,* Earthjustice, http://earthjustice.org/features/ourwork/timeline-monsanto-s-chemical-romance.

62816909R00121

Made in the USA
Lexington, KY
19 April 2017